Ethnic Embroidery

Ethnic Embroidery

An introduction with special reference to the embroidery of China, India, Palestine and Yugoslavia

MARGARET OHMS

B.T. Batsford Ltd, London

Acknowledgment

Many people helped in the making of this book. I wish to thank Judy Smith for the hours of help over many months; The owners of the embroideries; Auckland Institute and Museum, Yeshe Eastern Galleries, Loreen Benson, Beryl Brown, Sheridan Carter, Ivor and Patricia Durovich, Cate Frey, Alan and Rita Graham, Mary Heslop, Muriel Hooper, Muriel Johnson, Pat McKay, Ann Neads, Ann Outwin, Jessie Pugh, Florence Richie, Jessie Segedin, Melanie Stewart, Grace Wong. The Photographers Roy Beck and Peter Ohms who made the text almost unnecessary.

Dedicated to the men and women, both unknown and forgotten, who, for various reasons, stitched the embroideries.

ISBN 0 8521 9739 X

Typeset by Servis Filmsetting Ltd.
and printed in Great Britain by
Jolly and Barber Ltd, Rugby,
bound by Anchor Press, Tiptree

for the Publishers
B.T. Batsford Ltd
4 Fitzhardinge St
London W1H 0AH

British Library Cataloguing in Publication Data

Ohms, Margaret
   Ethnic embroidery: an introduction with
   special reference to the Embroidery of
   China, India, Palestine & Yugoslavia.
   1. Embroidery
   I. Title
   746.44

Black and white photography by Peter Ohms

Colour photography by Roy Beck

Contents

Introduction

Throughout history there has been a continual movement of people, emigrating of their own free will or being forcibly moved by wars and frontier changes, or sometimes just as far as the next valley through marriage. They took with them the remembered stitches and patterns of their homelands and possibly their embroidered garments and household linen. In the years that followed, the patterns were often forgotten; the hard new life was not conducive to such things as embroidery. But now, several generations later, there is a new awareness, and grandchildren want to learn the patterns and stitches of their cultural heritage. As well as this, and perhaps of even greater importance, is the fact that the people they now live amongst want to know and understand more about the culture of their neighbours.

The embroideries described in this book are almost all of the type that can be found in the community. Many are treasured possessions brought as a memory of home when the family emigrated. Others have been idly collected by travellers or people working in foreign countries who may have some knowledge of how they were worked.

The stitches all look vaguely familiar, but the colour combinations are often strange to our eyes, and the patterns barely understood. Yet all have a fascinating story to tell.

1

What is embroidery?

Embroidery is a general term used for the enriching or ornamentation of cloth using a needle and thread. It is usually worked on a woven fabric, but the term also applies to work made on skins and felt. Sometimes the work is further enriched by the addition of shells, beads, mirrors, metallic threads or wires or other fabrics. From earliest times man has had a compulsive urge to decorate his clothes and other possessions, often with embroidery, but because of the perishable nature of fabric very few examples survive – some double running stitch from the dry sands of Peru, a sampler fragment from Egypt, some appliqué from the permafrost of Mongolia, and some coloured whipping stitches from the peat bogs of north Germany.

Some of the carved designs on stone and wooden statues of antiquity suggest embroidered patterns, and there are written accounts of 'embroidery', but the word is often used loosely, to describe patterns in weaving. Sometimes, however, the weaving was altered or complemented by the use of a needle and thread, and this can be regarded as true embroidery. Just as there is confusion about the so-called *Bayeux Tapestry* of 1066, which is not a tapestry, but a true embroidery, so there is even more confusion about early descriptions of embroidery. There is no way of knowing whether the descriptions were of weaving, embroidery copying weaving, or weaving assisted by some embroidery stitches. In all probability, embroidery developed from this original 'assistance' to weaving, although it is possible that it developed with garment-makers who worked with skins, and later with fabrics, and needed special stitches along seams that would hold the pieces, reinforce the weakened cut edge, and, as a bonus, be decorative. Whatever the true story of its development, whether by the weaver or the tailor, it was always worked by an artisan who had an intimate working knowledge of his materials. Embroidery can be placed into two main groups, free and counted. In 'free' embroidery the stitches move at will over the background material, be it skin, felt, or finely-woven cloth. In counted embroidery, the nature of the woven background material determines the size and direction of the stitches, and to some extent the pattern. Where there is a strong tailoring tradition, there is often a predominance of free embroidery, but where coarser fabrics were woven, there tends to be a close bond with counted work.

FIG 1 Detail from a Chamba rumal or covering cloth of birds and garlands, the embroidery curving freely over the background fabric. Worked in silk floss in long split stitch. Chamba region of Himalayas, early twentieth century

Ethnic embroidery, whether free or counted, is the embroidery of specific peoples and regions, their particular mix of colour, stitch and pattern becoming as distinctive as a signature. It is the embroidery of isolation, but uses borrowings from everywhere. It is usually worked with some purpose in view, on clothing and household linen, for identification and display, and especially for the 'Rites of Passage', the ceremonial trappings associated with birth, marriage and death. Embroidery is not universal. Some places are famous for their work; in others it is rare or non-existent. The Arabic proverb, 'Embroidery signifies a lack of work', suggests that if women worked long hours in the fields they had little time for embroidery, but this disregards the work done by women after the husbandry was finished; by the men and women eking out a living by embroidering in small village workshops, and later co-operatives, and by the slightly more prosperous villagers who had some leisure. In countries where there were embroidery workshops attached to the court, or organised cottage industries, styles of work and techniques gradually filtered down and influenced the work of the ordinary villagers.

With the Industrial Revolution, which caused redundancy of

FIG 2 Detail from a cloth of cypress trees, counted over two threads in cross stitch. The slope and size of the stitches is dictated by the background and the motifs are angular in shape. Palestine, modern

cottage industry embroiderers, while at the same time introducing the mass production of cheap household textiles, ethnic embroidery declined. This decline was emphasised by improved and speedier travel and communication, which destroyed the isolation of many ethnic groups. Until this time, isolation had played a dominant role in preserving the uniqueness of various types of embroidery. In a world where it is possible to fly from Auckland to London in one day, we tend to forget how isolated people were even at the beginning of the twentieth century. A trip that today we think nothing of making in order to do some casual shopping, could, at walking pace, take a whole day. Even where there were roads, there were often no bridges. Once, when I asked some Hungarian immigrants how it was that there was such a diversity in their embroidery styles, they looked at me in disbelief and in halting English explained, 'the mountains were so high, the rivers so wide'.

Of course there has always been some transfer of patterns, with marriage linking distant family groups, and there was always 'stealing by eye', the copying of patterns from anywhere and everywhere. A Polish woman described to me how as a child she had watched a farm cart laden with household linen slowly make its way from one outlying farm to another on the other side of the village, how it had seemed to slow within sight of the houses, and how the curtains fluttered almost imperceptibly as it passed by. Just as has happened with certain styles in architecture, so embroidery began to acquire a universal sameness. But recently there has been a growing awareness of ethnic identity, as well as a willingness to understand other people's cultures. Some may argue that by using and adapting ethnic patterns, we will further destroy their distinctive styles. This is not necessarily true. By understanding more fully the nature of the materials and threads used, and how they influenced the final work, we will increase our appreciation of the underlying significance of the motifs and the ways in which the limited number of stitches were used. The more we understand about the true nature of ethnic embroidery, the more likely we are to treasure and conserve the little that remains.

2

Characteristics of ethnic embroidery

Every piece of ethnic embroidery is unique; many distinguishing features combine to make this so. The most important of these are: background material, threads, type of work, stitches used, colour, motif, design, placement, and use.

Background material

The original fabrics, whether linen, cotton, silk, or wool, were those indigenous to the particular region. In addition, a limited number of skins, both fish and animal, were used, and small amounts of other plant fibres, such as hemp. In many cases, the textile fibre was actually home-grown, as well as home-spun and woven. Studies of linen production in Scandinavia suggest that as long as eighteen months was needed for the cycle from seed and and sowing to harvest, spinning, and finally weaving. Spinning and weaving alone took a considerable time. The need to prepare the fibre for weaving, and then to watch the weft threads cross over and under the warp as the weaving progressed, gave the weaver an insight into the structure and properties of the finished cloth that, if the weave was of sufficient weight, made counting a pattern on to the fabric second nature. Homewoven fabric could vary from the incredibly fine, even by today's standards, and so unsuitable for counted work, to the heavier, more textured cloth on which the pattern was usually counted. Modern fabrics have a rounded thread and an appreciable space between the threads, which makes counting easier – something quite foreign to the closely-packed, flattened threads of earlier fabrics. The weight of warp and weft threads could also vary quite considerably. Present-day embroiderers often feel that it is not possible to satisfactorily count a pattern on to a fabric with a variable thread size, not understanding that when the loom is set up, the thread count, inch by inch, will be consistent, however much the individual threads vary. The slight unevenness in this sort of fabric gives to the embroidery an interesting quality that is absent when work is done on a less textured fabric.

Threads

The earliest threads used for embroidery were linen, silk, and wool. Like the fabric, these are all perishable, even under the best conditions. As they were subjected to wear and tear, moth, mould, sunlight or neglect, it is not surprising that very little fabric and thread has been found belonging to the era before ours, ending 2000 years ago. In all cases that which has been found suggests a long history of spinning and weaving going back into antiquity. Decorated spindle whorls made of clay and stone from as early as Neolithic times have been found in large numbers, along with many loom weights and sometimes small fragments of both plaited and woven fabrics. Various dates have been arrived at for the discovery of thread and its use in weaving: 6000 BC for linen, 4000 BC for wool, 2700 BC for silk. These dates can be only approximate, and it is very likely that they will be revised to further back in time as further archaeological evidence becomes available. Although cotton was known to have been woven as early as 3000 BC it did not become important as a thread for sewing until after AD 1800. Before this date the technology needed to make the cotton yarn strong enough to take the tension required in sewing had not been developed. In rural areas, homespun thread for family use continued to be made until relatively recently. Some ethnic embroidery, particularly counted work, appears to be worked with a much heavier thread than we find acceptable today. This tends to give a bold, almost over-stuffed look. In free work much use was made of silk floss, a fine thread with a minimum of twist.

Type of work – free or counted

The type of fabric used greatly influenced the embroidery. Counted work, such as pattern darning, is so closely related to weaving that it may have developed as a short cut to produce a complicated weaving pattern. When the background material has an obvious warp and

FIG 3 Pattern darning. Detail from a cloth, red pearl thread on white fabric, 10 threads/cm (24 threads/in). The stitches lie beside the warp threads and the pattern could have been woven instead of stitched. Yugoslavia, modern

weft, the spaces between the threads were used to position either straight or diagonal stitches. This regulated both the size and slope of the stitch and dictated the range of geometrical shapes, as is seen in Hardanger and counted satin stitch. In cross stitch, the pattern can become even more closely tied to the fabric, so much so that in one-colour designs the background can become as important as the counted pattern.

Fabrics without an obvious weave are more suited to free work, the fabric serving as a backdrop to as well as a support for, the stitches. In some Middle Eastern countries, counted work is used on fabrics such as cotton sateen and crepe on which, because of their special weave, it is not possible to count. The problem is solved by embroidering the design over a countable fabric, or canvas, stitched to the original fabric. When the embroidery is completed, the canvas is painstakingly frayed out, leaving the counted motif. Originally, these counted patterns had been embroidered on heavier, countable homespun. With the advent of finer machine-made fabric, the old patterns were not put aside, but instead a compromise method of working evolved.

FIG 4 Geometrical or counted satin stitch. Detail from a cloth, counted over the linen in a traditional star shape. The motifs tend to look heavy and so the design has been lightened by blocks of background showing through the stitched motif. Cyprus, mid twentieth century

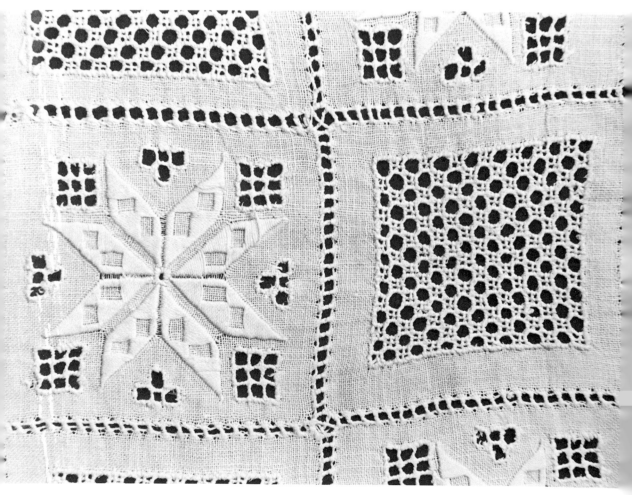

FIG 5 Counted satin stitch. Detail from a cloth, white stranded cotton on yellow fabric. The satin stitches are worked in stepped blocks and the background plays a very important part in the design. Yugoslavia, modern

FIG 6 Cross stitch and stroke stitch. Detail from a cloth, red pearl thread on cotton, showing an all-over pattern where the background tends to dominate the worked pattern. Palestine, Morocco modern

Stitches

Stitches depend on the background material for support, and in the case of counted work for their form. Thus the type of fabric available influences the choice of stitch. For weavers, straight stitches that followed the warp and weft were an obvious choice. These could be arranged in a variety of ways to imitate complicated weaving patterns (pattern darning), or they could be worked in blocks of parallel stitches (Hardanger; counted satin stitch). A much simpler effect could be achieved by counting a single running stitch over the warps and weft, and filling in the spaces left on the return journey (double running).

When stitches lying on a regular slope were used, we find all the varieties of cross stitch, tent and gobelin stitch. Curved lines were not possible, but an illusion of a curve could be obtained by double running or back stitch used in conjunction with both cross stitch and satin stitch. On the other hand, the stitches that could be used on a background that demanded little were endless. The pattern could

FIG 7 Stroke stitch, a form of double running, follows the warp threads but crosses them diagonally on the return journey. Sudan, mid twentieth century

FIG 8 Detail from a cloth. Double running stitch used with counted satin stitch to give an illusion of a curve. Spain, mid twentieth century

curve at will, and some stitches were particularly suited to this use, especially for outlines (chain stitch, outline stitch, feather stitch). Where there was a need to fill in large areas economically, stitches that lay on the surface with little thread on the back evolved as in laid work, Cretan stitch, Oriental stitch and herring bone stitch. Oriental stitch is particularly ingenious, as the laid thread is attached at the completion of each stitch. Of the wide variety of stitches available, different ethnic groups tend to use just a few, often in their own particular way.

FIG 9 Detail from a cloth. Back stitch used with counted satin stitch and cut work and giving the appearance of a curve. Italy, mid twentieth century

FIG 10 Detail from a bed cover of large areas of silk floss floated over the surface of the handwoven linen and attached with rows of couched threads. Portugal, late nineteenth century

FIG 11 Detail from the front of an export trade skirt. Worked in white, brown and yellow on red cotton fabric, in chain stitch, shisha stitch and closed herringbone stitch. Herringbone stitch is commonly used in India. It is one of several stitches used to economise on thread, as the back shows

FIG 12 Detail of the back of Fig 11. India, modern

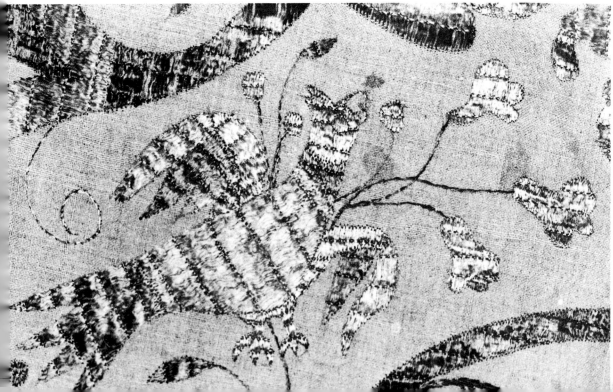

Use of colour

Colour must have always been a luxury. The earliest evidence of colour dyestuffs in fabrics comes from fragments dating from Neolithic times, and was of three colours: yellow, red and blue. It is recorded that the art of dyeing was practised in China about 3000 BC, that madder and indigo were used in India from 2500 BC, and that cloth still showing traces of yellow, green, red and blue have been found with mummy wrappings in Egyptian tombs dating from 2000 BC, but these dyes were all found in fabrics from the tombs of important or even royal persons. Some dyestuffs were actually set aside for the sole use of the nobility; saffron was a royal colour in early Greece; Tyrian purple was reserved for the robes of emperors, consuls, and chief magistrates in Rome; in China during the Manchu dynasty, yellow was for the sole use of the emperor and his consort.

Wool and cotton have natural colour variations. Cotton varies from dingy white to brown, while wool ranges from cream through fawn to browns and almost black. This range in wool colouring was almost certainly exploited then as it is now. The dyeing of fibres entails considerable work, and expertise, for while wool and silk are protein fibres and accept dyes readily, cotton and linen are cellulose and so are difficult to dye.

Of the classic dyestuffs of antiquity, indigo, madder, safflower and saffron were probably the best known, Indigo produced a blue dye which was used extensively in embroidery as it was known in Asia and around the Mediterranean. Madder was cultivated for the red dye that was obtained from its roots and was found mainly in tropical areas, while safflower, which also produced a red dye, was more widespread, being native to parts of Asia, central India to the Middle East and Ethiopia. Saffron, a golden yellow dye, comes from the saffron crocus, which is believed to be native to the Mediterranean, Asia Minor, and Iran, and was long cultivated in Iran and Kashmir. In isolated areas, the availability of dyes would depend on which plants grew locally, and to a lesser extent on the distance to the nearest trade routes.

In Europe and the Middle East, household linen and much clothing was woven from cotton and linen, both hard to dye, so it is small wonder that a large amount of embroidery on these articles was done with natural-coloured threads. Another group of ethnic embroidery designs are worked in just one colour, black, dark blue, or red, while a third group is worked in two colours often red and blue or red and black. The fourth main group made use of several colours, up to eight in number, but these were straight colours, not shades of the same colour. Even with a limited range, great use was made of colour to carry the eye forward along a design. The edging (Fig 13a) is from a Yugoslavian embroidery in two colours; two small angled motifs in blue are followed by two in red. The eye is enticed to look further along the border as it jumps to the next block of red, and then to the next. The same sort of thing happens in Fig 13b, an edging from Palestine. Here the red edging is tipped with black, but after every five black stitches two are left plain, so that the eye automatically jumps to the next group of five stitches. Another commonly-used

FIG 13a Edging pattern from the collar band of an *oshvitza*, worked in red and blue cross stitch. Montenegro, mid twentieth century

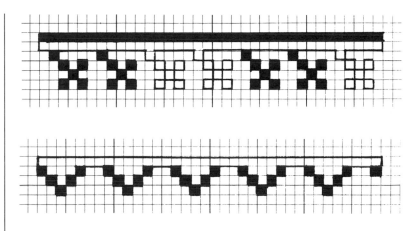

FIG 13b Edging from the Jerusalem sampler (Fig 50) worked in red and black. Mid twentieth century

method is to alternate several colours, so that the eye is led by colour right into the following motif. By arranging half of a motif in a contrasting colour, a turning windmill effect may be achieved.

Although the range of colours in ethnic embroidery was often limited, the colours that were available were used to give maximum impact, and colours that to our eyes appear to 'clash' were placed side by side with stunning results.

In the wake of the Industrial Revolution much experimentation was carried out in order to produce cheap dyestuffs synthetically. Eventually the first synthetic dye was produced in about 1860, but as late as 1900, indigo dye, the dyestuff of working-mens clothes and of every pair of blue jeans, was still obtained almost entirely from the indigo plant, with India as the main source of supply. Where embroiderers bought manufactured thread, synthetic dyes eventually replaced the old vegetable dyes, but where they spun and dyed their own thread, the change took place much more slowly.

Motifs and the build-up of design

Embroidery designs are built up in different ways. The basic unit of a design is called a motif. Motifs can vary from strictly geometrical and close to the straight stitches of the original weavers, to realistic motifs in free work. If a motif is used on its own, it is called a *spot motif* (Fig 14).

An embroidery design may be made up of a collection of different spot motifs arranged over an area, or *field*, which is surrounded by a border or series of borders, or there may be only one spot motif used with variations in colour or in the direction in which it lies. This arrangement is very common in some Indian embroideries. However, the majority of patterns consist of motifs, side by side, linked together in a repeating pattern. The link is often no more than a line, sometimes straight, sometimes undulating and intricate. A design may be made up of the same motif repeated endlessly along a line and at right angles to it (Fig 15a) or slightly different (Fig 15b) or completely different motifs may alternate (Fig 15c). The motifs may grow out from the main line diagonally (Fig 15d), or they may be arranged on either side of a vertical line, like the branches of a tree

FIG 14 Detail from a jacket.
Spot motifs embroidered
with polycoloured silk floss
on handwoven raw silk in
stem stitch and Oriental
stitch. Kashmir, mid
twentieth century

FIG 15 Arrangement of
motifs linked with a straight
line

22

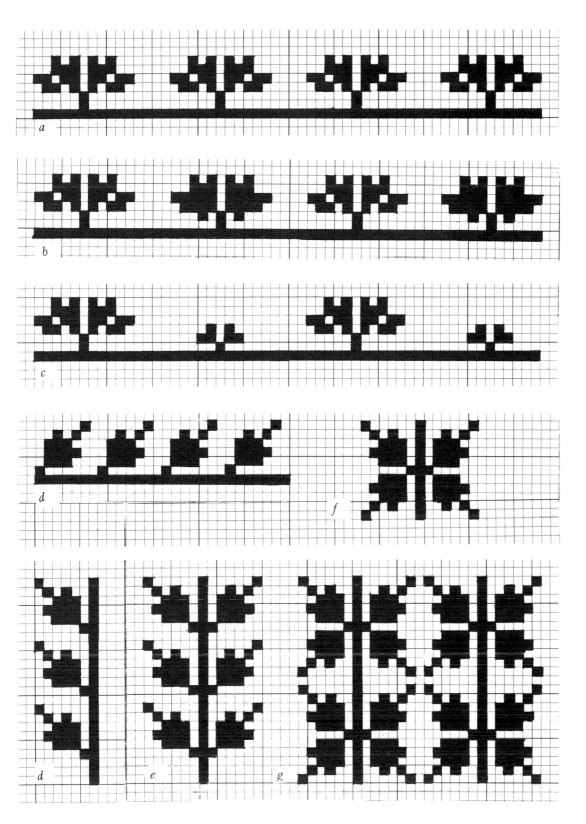

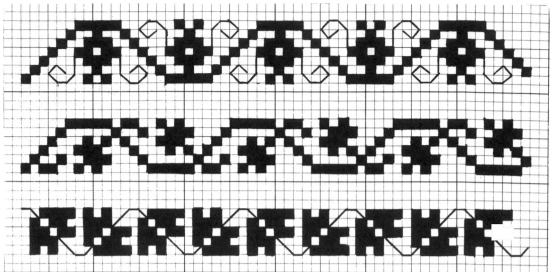

FIG 16 Motifs linked along
an undulating line

FIG 17 Detail from a shirt,
muslin embroidered with
indigo stranded cotton, the
design flowing with the line.
Satin stitch, coral stitch, fly
stitch and detached chain
stitch. Design adapted from
an eighteenth-century
Indian woodblock

24

FIG 18 Detail from a cloth. Corded silk embroidered in chain stitch with twisted silk thread. The line has turned back on itself into a figure of eight and the crossing is covered with the main motif. Persia, early twentieth century

(Fig 15e). Using the same motif and its mirror image, compound block motifs can be formed (Fig 15f) and these can be arranged to produce all-over designs (Fig 15g). Designs built around an undulating line are even more numerous. The motifs may be placed at right angles to the direction of the line or flow with it, or from it (Figs 16, 17). Sometimes the line turns back on itself and the motif becomes enclosed in the space produced (Fig 18).

Breakdown of design

It is surprisingly difficult to make an exact copy of a free work design. Each time the motif is repeated, slight changes occur, even when the embroidery is worked by the original designer. When the pattern is reproduced by others, the most astonishing changes can take place, until with time the motif becomes almost unrecognisable. These changes can be caused by a lack of technical ability on the part of the worker, or by a lack of understanding of the nature of the motif, or simply by careless workmanship. Many lotus flowers in Chinese embroidery have become so conventionalised that they often look more like peonies, and even appear with peony leaves.

Fig 19 shows a detail from an ari of Ganesh, the elephant headed

FIG 19 Detail from an ari of
Ganesh, the elephant headed
Hindu god, worked in chain
stitch with silk on cotton.
India, second half twentieth
century

FIG 20 Detail from an
embroidery showing Ganesh
in an almost unrecognisable
form. Second half twentieth
century

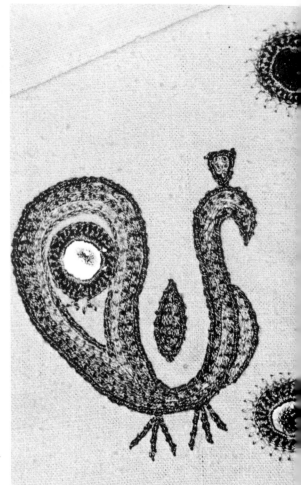

FIG 21 Detail from an ari, chain stitched with silk on cotton. The wing is still attached to the body. India, second half twentieth century

FIG 22 Detail from a jacket, worked in shisha stitch, chain stitch, whipped chain stitch and buttonhole stitch. The wing has moved to the space between the neck and tail and is now unrecognisable

Indian god of prudence and farsightedness. Ganesh is usually depicted coloured red with a pot belly and four arms that hold a noose, a goad, a pot of sweetmeats or rice and, lastly, his broken tusk. In the ari hanging, Ganesh would be instantly recognisable by anyone who had lived in India, but in the second Ganesh embroidery, the god is almost unrecognisable (Fig 20). It is true that Ganesh has been stitched in red, but now the trunk grows oddly from his forehead, two arms have been lost, and the stool on which he is seated now looks more like a mat. This breakdown of design has also occurred with the two peacocks. In Fig 21 the wing is in an odd position, but still attached to the body, while in Fig 22 the wing has become reduced in proportion to the size of the body and has moved to the space between the neck and tail. The legs are reduced to feet. At the base of each otherwise symmetrical motif in the Chikan cloth (Fig 23) there is a small, unnecessary grace note. There are dozens of this particular motif, all worked in the same way, so it is obviously meant to be there and is not a one-off mistake. The patterns for the Chikan work are printed on muslin with a greased wooden block which must also have

carried the little mark. Persian woven textiles of the early seventeenth century often show motifs with an asymmetrical root or flower and it is interesting to speculate whether this small stitch is a remnant of a memory from long ago (Fig 24a,b).

In counted work, it is quite easy to reproduce a design if there is a pattern to follow, but workers in ethnic embroidery tended to work patterns from memory and so they were rarely, if ever, set down. Patterns were also copied incorrectly and this makes the graphs from the almond pattern from Palestinian embroidery rather interesting. They are too alike to be unrelated, they both appear in embroidery of the same period, but in Fig 25 the tendril has joined the stem, and the almond has gained a tip. The lotus flower designs from neighbouring provinces in western China are also interesting. Usually, when a cross stitch pattern is worked on an undulating framework, any 'leaves' and 'tendrils' are placed within the framework beside the flower as in Fig 26a, but in Fig 26b the 'tendrils' have migrated and now sit outside the traditional framework.

Designs can also appear to be altered by the use of different colour

FIG 23 Detail from a cloth worked in white cotton on fine white muslin, showing the small, almost symmetrical motif, (enlarged in Fig 152). India, first half twentieth century

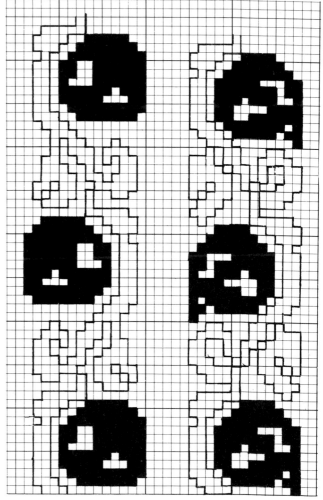

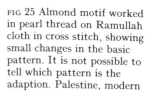
FIG 25 Almond motif worked
in pearl thread on Ramullah
cloth in cross stitch, showing
small changes in the basic
pattern. It is not possible to
tell which pattern is the
adaption. Palestine, modern

FIG 24a Asymmetric root on
plant form drawn from a
woven silk double cloth.
Early seventeenth century

FIG 24b Asymmetric root in
the form of a flower, drawn
from a brocaded silk velvet.
Persia, seventeenth century

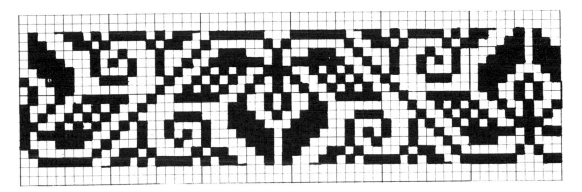

FIG 26a Lotus design, 1920

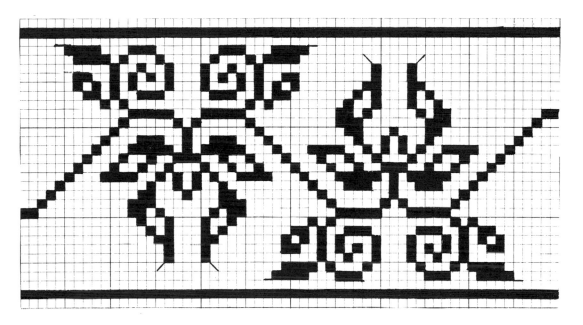

FIG 26b Lotus design from
Kuiechou province, 1930

emphasis, even though the arrangement of stitches remains the same. While many traditional cross stitch patterns are worked in one colour and depend upon the interplay of this colour with the background material to such an extent that they would be spoiled by the introduction of a second colour, there are also many patterns that do not have this dependence. These patterns can be changed quite simply, though radically, by substituting different colours. In the pattern from a Palestinian chest panel, colour has been used in a rather unusual way. The basic pattern is made from a simple flower and leaf motif which faces first left, and then right, to form a broken but undulating line (Fig 27). In the 1950 chest panel, two leaves and a flower have been emphasised (Fig 27b); in a 1910 sleeve pattern it has been arranged as in Fig 27c; while on headgear from the same date the pattern has been changed again and appears as in Fig 27d.

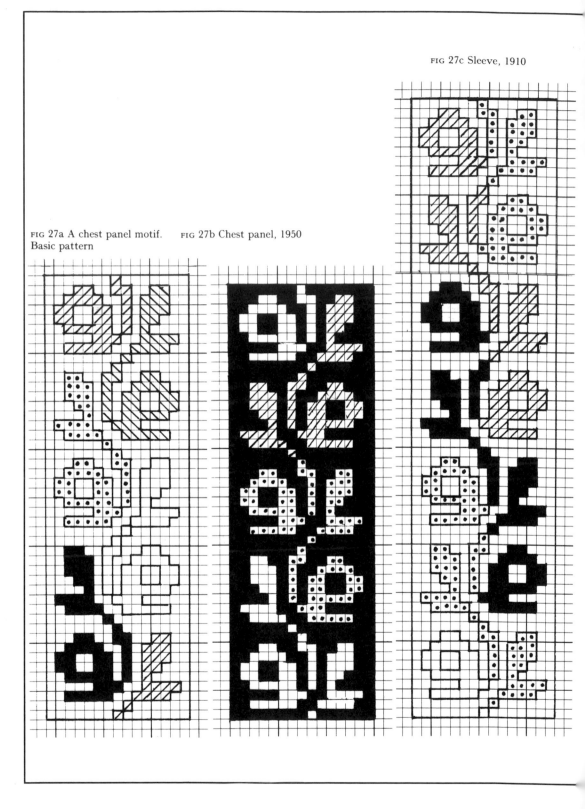

FIG 27c Sleeve, 1910

FIG 27a A chest panel motif.   FIG 27b Chest panel, 1950
Basic pattern

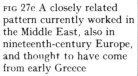

FIG 27e A closely related
pattern currently worked in
the Middle East, also in
nineteenth-century Europe,
and thought to have come
from early Greece

FIG 27d Headgear pattern
adaption, 1910

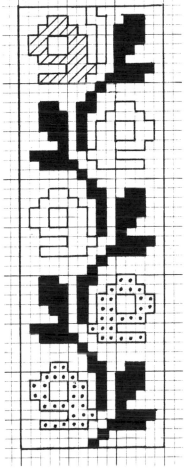

Placement of embroidery

Although embroidery was sometimes used to completely cover a fabric (Fig 28), it was more often worked along seams and used to finish edges (Fig 29). This was especially true of household linen, while on garments these edges became hems, cuffs, and neck openings. When the early tailors stitched skins together to make garments, the weakest part was along the seam. Decorative stitches are thought to have been worked along this line of weakness, to give both extra strength and ornament. When garments were made from woven cloth, the problems were different. Woven cloth is very strong along its edge or selvedge, but is weakened considerably by cutting. If a garment consisted of a long loom length of cloth wound round the body, the cut edges could be tied into a strong fringe and so there was no problem. Some early looms, however, were narrow and garments from these were constructed by joining together pieces of cloth for extra width. If at all possible this was done selvedge to selvedge, with

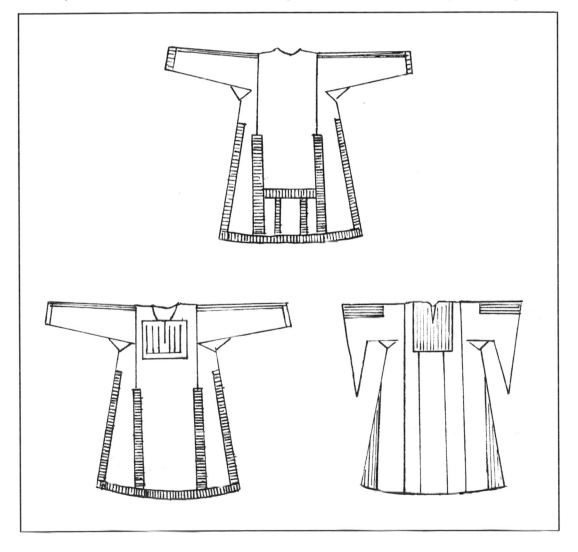

35

FIG 30 Detail from a 1910 Bethlehem wedding dress. Extra width has been added to the dress by silk side panels which have been joined by stitches in silk floss. The motifs are made from couched cords, the spaces filled with satin stitch in silk floss

a minimum of cutting, a feature being made of the join and, in the case of Palestinian dresses, extra embroidered panels were added along the seams (Figs 30, 31). Even when larger looms made the addition of extra material unnecessary, the fabric was cut to the old width and the decorative seams and panels then added. Neck openings and chest panels were probably the most important areas for embroidery. Many people believed that evil forces could enter the body with disastrous consequences, the head, neck and chest being the most vulnerable, and thus in greatest need of protection. This protection was given in several ways, by charms, talismans, richly embroidered bands and chest panels. In Indian embroidery, powerful protection against evil spirits was given when little shisa glass mirrors were sewn to garments and household articles. Evil spirits, seeing their reflection in the mirrors, were supposed to take flight and flee from sight (Fig 32).

FIG 31 Detail from a shirt, natural-coloured hand-woven linen. The seam has been controlled with a four-sided stitch and hem stitch and further enriched with needle weaving in natural, red and blue. The geometrical satin stitch is worked in linen thread. Eastern Mediterranean, early twentieth century

Use of designs with modern threads and colours

Often, modern designs adapted from older ethnic embroideries look wrong and out of place. This is brought about by several factors – the use of different threads, different fabrics, different colours, a changed scale of work, and sometimes the use of a different stitch.

Probably the most important of these is the thread. Modern threads are very different from the silk and linen threads that were once available. The silk was used, either as a floss, or as a heavily twisted thread, which gave an almost three-dimensional effect. Silk thread was used for embroidering on silk, but it was also used on linens and on cottons, such as calico. Much ethnic embroidery has this rich, heavy look, which Pearl threads capture to some extent. Fabrics, however, are not so difficult to match. The fabrics used ranged from silk and the finest muslins to heavy homespun and woven linens. The

37

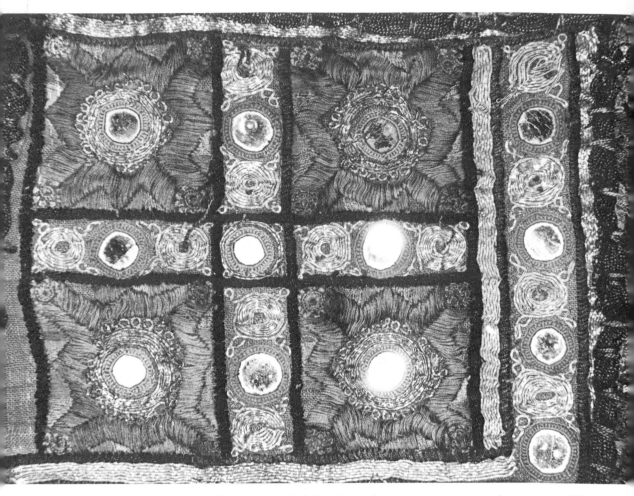

FIG 32 Detail from a *chakla* made from worn-out pieces of chest panels patched together and the seams covered with heavy couched threads. On the original chest panel, the *shisha* mirrors were used to frighten away evil spirits. India, second half twentieth century

homewoven fabrics showed some unevenness, and were very different from modern embroidery materials, which are woven with smooth, round, evenly-spaced threads. Then, the colours used depended on which plants suitable for dyeing fabric were readily available; today, our colours are graded into a bewildering range, with sometimes as many as seven shades in one group. It is possible to get the effect of ethnic embroidery by using colours from several different brands of thread in the same piece of work. This will help to give the special quality that the modern co-ordinated colours deny. It is important to know in just what scale the patterns were worked; some fabrics were unbelievably fine; some were coarse and textured. A design worked on a 36 threads/inch (14 threads/cm) count may look crude and heavy on 18 threads/inch (7 threads/cm) fabric.

When ethnic embroidery is described, the term cross stitch is often used to describe what is in fact double-sided cross stitch or plait stitch. Both these stitches have a more substantial appearance than the more usual cross stitch. When cross stitch or plait stitch was worked in one colour, the direction of the stitch was often changed in part of the pattern, to catch the light and give the effect of another colour being used. The old embroideries vary in technique and workmanship just as much as modern work; some work is fine and painstakingly done, while other work is rough and careless. In counted work the first motif was counted, but subsequent ones were usually marked out with a needle, which often led to a variation in motifs in the same piece of embroidery. In fact motifs vary considerably, and when graphing up patterns it is sometimes impossible to find two exactly alike. The overall effect still appears surprisingly uniform, but it has a different look from the machinelike quality we expect today.

Free-work patterns were sometimes printed on the fabric with ink, or, in the case of chikankari, with greased blocks, which were sometimes drawn on by a local person who was good at drawing. Some of these designers were more famous than the actual embroiderers, for their names have been recorded while those of the workers have been forgotten. In the court workshops of China, professional designers used stencils as well as free drawing. Whatever the method of putting the design on the fabric, and however good the design, in the end the success of the embroidery, then as now, depended on the thought, interpretation, and workmanship of the embroiderer.

3
China

FIG 33 Detail from a collar worked in polycoloured silk in brick stitch over gauze, 14 threads/cm (36 threads/in). The motifs are outlined with couched gold thread. China, late nineteenth century

FIG 34 Enlarged detail of Fig 36. The type of gauze used can be seen between the brick stitch and the edge of the binding

Overleaf
FIG 35 Detail from a sleeve band. Water is indicated with long stem stitch, pine tree in straight stitch, all worked in twisted silk thread. Pine trees along with bamboo and willows often appear on sleeve bands. The pine and bamboo were both evergreen and symbolised longevity. China, late nineteenth century

FIG 36 Detail from embroidery of a phoenix, the symbol of the Empress, with tree peony flowers in polycoloured silk, worked in long tailed Chinese knots and outlined with couched gold thread. China, nineteenth century

China is an immense country, with an area of over $9\frac{1}{2}$ million square kilometres. It borders on Russia and Mongolia in the north, and on Vietnam, Burma and India in the west. Over the centuries various ethnic groups have filtered into the country, bringing their particular embroidery styles, but the rich silk and gold embroidery of the Imperial Court has so dominated the embroidery scene that it comes as a surprise to find pieces from some of the outlying provinces using cross and double running stitches on hand-woven cotton. The textile history of China has for thousands of years been bound up with the production of silk, a protein fibre unwound from the cocoon of the silkworm.

Virtually all the traditional embroidery is free work, on silk fabric – either satin weave, or damask – a small amount is on gauze (Fig 33 and 34), and there is some counted work on cotton. While the thread count of the cotton ranges from 20–24 threads/cm (50–60 threads/in), the gauze count is 14–26 threads/cm (36–46 threads/in). The silk thread is used either twisted or as floss, the type of thread greatly influencing the style of embroidery used. Floss silk is extremely difficult to control and cannot be laid down over large areas without being attached to the base fabric by other stitches, a technique called 'laid work'.

Chinese embroidery uses few stitches, and, of these, satin stitch predominates, as it is ideally suited to the silk floss thread. Satin stitch is worked in the same way as the stitch that we know, but also as surface satin stitch, and as 'encroaching' or 'butted' satin stitch. Satin stitch and surface satin stitch are sometimes used indiscriminately on the same piece of work. To separate the units used in a design, e.g. petals in a flower, a technique called *voiding* is used, the petals being indicated not by outline, but by spaces. Satin stitch is also used as the base stitch in a special form of laid work that is then couched with a finer thread in a geometrical pattern. Small amounts of stem stitch are used for outlining (Fig 35), straight stitches to indicate leaves and flowers (Fig 35), couching for attaching the gold thread used for outlining motifs and filling backgrounds and Chinese knots, occasionally long tailed, are used as a filling stitch (Fig 36). Pekinese stitch is used brilliantly to control gold thread, and one wonders if it was invented just for that purpose. On gauze, brick and

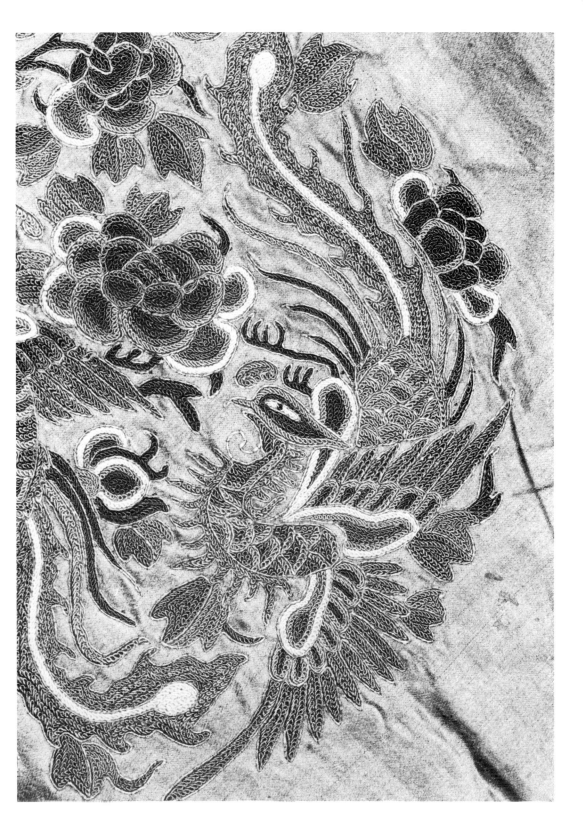

tent stitch are used to totally cover the fabric. It has been suggested that these two stitches arrived in China relatively recently and were due to European influences. In counted embroidery on fabric, cross stitch and double running were used. The examples here were collected in China in the early 1930s by missionaries working in the Kueichou province. They are worked on hand-woven cotton of narrow loom width, which is a feature of rural Chinese embroidery. The silk used is of very variable weight, suggesting that it has been hand-twisted. The hems have been turned to the front and embroidered with coloured silk floss, another characteristic of rural work (Figs 37, 38, 39).

The motifs in Chinese embroidery are full of symbolism. State robes and badges of office had to display special symbols, any remaining space being filled at the discretion of the designer, using clouds, bats, butterflies, good luck symbols, diaper and meander patterns. Empty spaces were abhored. The official court costume, which was worn by all at court and those in the government service, represented an ordered universe, but the symbolism was only complete when the coat was worn, the wearer's head above the material world of the coat representing the spiritual kingdom. The lower border of diagonal bands indicated deep water; above this the waves and spray were the homes of dragons. Deep water could also be indicated by two shades of gold thread, which gave a stunning shimmering effect when viewed by artificial light in the early hours before dawn, the time considered most auspicious for court functions. Rising from the water, in the centre and at the sides, were sacred mountains, or, in the case of insignia, crags or rocks.

Court robes also displayed dragons, and some or all of the twelve ornaments of antiquity, which signified authority and power. The emperor had the right to wear the complete set, the number permitted decreasing with the rank of the wearer. Square pictorial badges (Fig 40), which were worn on plain navy blue or black three-quarter length surcoats, distinguished the various ranks of civil and military officials appointed to serve the dragon throne. As well as water and rocks, these badges displayed pheasants, peacocks, quails and geese, or animals such as tigers, lions and leopards. The birds and animals, signifying civil and military orders respectively, were all embroidered facing the sun, which represented the emperor; overhead were clouds and various religious symbols, below were rocks and water.

FIG 40 Left side of a front badge of office worked in couched gold and Chinese knots in polycoloured silk floss. It shows deep water, part of a bird facing the sun, symbolising the Emperor, the bat, *fu*, for good luck, the state umbrella and the endless knot, both Buddhist Emblems of Happy Augury, and the chrysanthemum, the flower of autumn, all outlined with a single gold thread. China, nineteenth century

FIG 41 Badge of office worked in tent stitch in polycoloured silk on gauze, 18 stitches/cm (46 stitches/in). The badge shows calm water, clouds, rocky crags, a fifth-rank silver pheasant facing the sun, and the tree peony, chrysanthemum, plum blossom and orchid, the flower valued for its wonderful fragrance. The background is in a swastika field pattern, the swastika being an ancient symbol of luck. The pheasant is very loosely attached – the width of the white card indicates the size of the stitches used to attach it to the main ground. China, late nineteenth century

Because of the varied techniques used to work the squares, it is often difficult to distinguish one creature from another. Many birds had remarkably similar bodies and wings, and often they could only be told apart by their tail feathers. While differing techniques and embroiderers' lack of skill were responsible for some of the confusion, it could also have been deliberate, one animal being made to look like another of higher rank. Two insignia were embroidered for each coat: one was for the back, while the front one was in two pieces to allow for the coat opening. Usually the insignia were embroidered as a whole unit, but there are some instances of the bird that signified rank being worked separately and stitched loosely to the badge. While some of these may have been the badges of civil servants in a hurry for promotion through the state examination system, towards the end of the era of the dragon throne, officials could also gain promotion by bribery (Fig 41).

Of all the symbols appearing in Chinese embroidery, special mention must be made of one of the most used and best loved, that of *fu*, the bat. The Chinese character for happiness is also pronounced *fu*, hence a play on words. To have two bats, the emblem of the god of

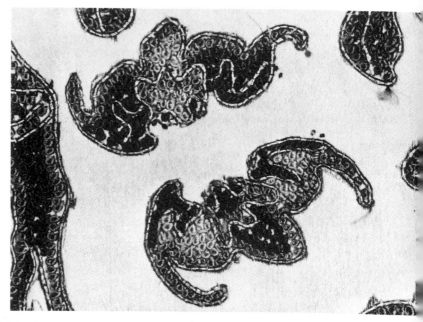

FIG 42 Enlarged detail from sleeve band of the bat, *fu*, worked in Chinese knots and outlined with couched gold thread. China, second half nineteenth century

FIG 43 Detail from a coat of chrysanthemum flowers worked in satin stitch and back stitch. China, modern

1. Detail from a sleeve band. Worked mainly in Chinese knots edged with couched gold thread. Above the hunter hover two bats, the emblem of the god of longevity and a very auspicious symbol, while by his feet grow the sacred fungus of immortality. China, late nineteenth century.

longevity, was even more auspicious, while five bats, not at all unusual in a piece of embroidery, signified health, wealth, long life, peace and happiness. Bats are sometimes so ornate that they bear a strong resemblance to butterflies, another much-used motif and the symbol of joy (Fig 42).

Some of the most beautiful of all embroidery was seen on women's informal robes and short coats. Here were embroidered a profusion of flowers – peony, magnolia, lotus, orchid, narcissus flower bulb and root, chrysanthemum and plum blossom. Possibly the most commonly-used were the tree peony, lotus, chrysanthemum and plum blossom, signifying respectively the coming of spring, summer, autumn, and winter (Fig 43). It is often hard to distinguish between an embroidered tree peony and a magnolia flower, as both have cupped and rounded petals, although fortunately their leaves are quite distinctive. It is not unusual to find in an embroidery lotus type flowers with pointed petals, but magnolia leaves. The lotus had been introduced into China, and was not nearly so well-known as the tree peony and magnolia, which were both native flowers. While it is obvious that some designers and embroiderers were familiar with the plants they were representing, others had possibly never seen the plant actually growing.

In 1912 thousands of years of silk culture and embroidery came to an end with the collapse of the Dragon Throne, triggered by foreign intervention in a country top-heavy with bureaucracy and civil servants, and by the decadence and isolation of the court. For the next fifty years China was wracked by wars and turmoil, and only recently has there been a resurgence of traditional embroidery.

4

India

Although the Indian Empire of the British Raj is now partitioned into Pakistan in the west and India in the east, and Afghanistan is autonomous, the embroidery of these three countries is still closely linked and difficult to separate. This is due partly to the far-reaching Moghul influence, which from around AD 1500 onwards, spread first from Persia to Afghanistan and then to north-west India, and to a lesser extent to the movements of nomadic peoples wandering across frontiers, following their livestock. Just as at present there is a mass movement of tribal and displaced people fleeing to Pakistan from the war in Afghanistan, taking with them their traditional patterns and textile skills, so in the past, styles of embroidery and traditional patterns moved from state to state.

Other outside influences were few, as the mountains to the north and east hampered contact with neighbouring peoples until the arrival of the European influence to the eastern seaboard. In 1600 the Moghul rulers of the Gujarat state gave the East India Company permission to set up a trading post at Surat. Initially the trade was in spices, but it soon expanded to include a flood of cotton textiles with new words to describe them: calico, chintz, madras, khaki, and dungaree. There also followed an interchange of ideas that enriched the embroidery worlds not only of Europe and America, but also of India itself. Much Indian embroidery is done by men working in small workshops, but it is the women at home, embroidering dowry clothes for their daughters, who have nurtured the embroidery tradition.

Historically, India is linked with the production of cotton, and it is in fact believed to be the oldest cotton growing country. The cotton plant, which belongs to the mallow family, grows naturally in India and it is believed to have been introduced from there into the Mediterranean area by Arab traders en route from India. There is archaeological evidence to suggest the cotton fabric from Sind was imported by Egyptians and later by the Greeks and Romans. The cotton fibres which surround the seeds of the plant have a very short staple – 2–6cm ($\frac{1}{2}$–2$\frac{1}{2}$in) – but because the fibres are twisted and have an uneven surface, they can be spun easily into yarn.

Almost all Indian embroidery is free work on cotton, either plain weave, or a special double weave called *Dusatti*. A small amount of silk is used, as well as wool, particularly in Kashmir. The threads used

2. Detail of the centre of a
Chamba rumal or covering
cloth. Worked in silk floss in
long split stitch and all the
thread lying on the surface
of the fabric. It shows the
milkmaids or *gopis* dancing
in a circle around the god
Krishna. Chamba region of
Himalayas, early twentieth
century.

3. Detail from an ari,
showing a band of borders
worked in chain stitch on
brown cotton with twisted
silk thread. The top border
is very similar to the lotus
borders of Egypt 4,000 years
ago. India

are cotton, silk floss, roughly twisted silk and 2-ply crewel wool, as well as metallic threads of gold and silver. Many different stitches are used, and these include satin stitch, stem stitch, couching, buttonhole stitch, long split stitch (Fig 44), Turkmen stitch, Oriental stitch, darning and chain stitch. Of these, chain stitch must be the most commonly associated with Indian embroidery, if for no reason other than the large production of crewel-work furnishing fabrics and the export trade in Numdah rugs, both of which are worked in chain stitch.

Chain stitch is thought to be one of the oldest stitches in the world. A small bird worked on silk in chain stitch was found in a fifth century BC tomb in China, while another possible example of chain stitch has been found in a German burial mound of about 530 BC, a find of great interest, considering the perishable nature of textiles. From China, where it is now almost forgotten, chain stitch spread to Persia and thence to India.

Chain stitch can be worked in three different ways, and because it is often called after its method of working, this can be very confusing. Chain stitch with a needle, tambouring, and ari work produce the same stitch. In India, the least commonly worked chain stitch is that

FIG 44 Detail from a chakla, worked in long split stitch and outlined in double running on black sateen. All the thread is lying on the surface. India, early twentieth century

FIG 45 Detail from a cloth, fine crewel wool on cotton in chain stitch of kingfisher fishing, in pink and off-white strips. Kashmir

worked with a needle, which is the one we in the West are most familiar with. Next in importance is tambouring. This method takes its name from the tambour, a drum-shaped frame over which the fine white muslin is stretched. The chain stitches were worked with a tambour hook at great speed, and, where possible, in continuous lines to avoid unnecessary beginnings and endings. In about 1760 tambouring was introduced into Europe, where it became very popular, but it was still worked in India as late as 1900. While English and French designs were mostly just outlined and very delicate, Indian work often featured Indian motifs and, being filled in, had a heavier look.

By far the most common method of working chain stitch is with an ari. This tool is like a small cobbler's awl, and is used without a frame, the design being worked from the top, away from the worker. It can be worked with a twisted silk thread, but is more commonly worked with crewel wool. Much ari work is made up of motifs on a plain ground, but if the fabric is to be completely covered with stitches, the motifs are worked first, and the background then filled in with a series of long lines of chain stitch, following the outline of the various motifs, or with a series of whorls (Figs 45, 46).

After ari work, the embroidery worked most in India is probably *shisha* work. *Shisha* is the Hindustani word for 'glass' or 'mirror'. While ari work is the work of the men in the professional workshops, *shishadur* is the embroidery of the village and tribal women. It is considered to be a true folk art, and has changed little over the years.

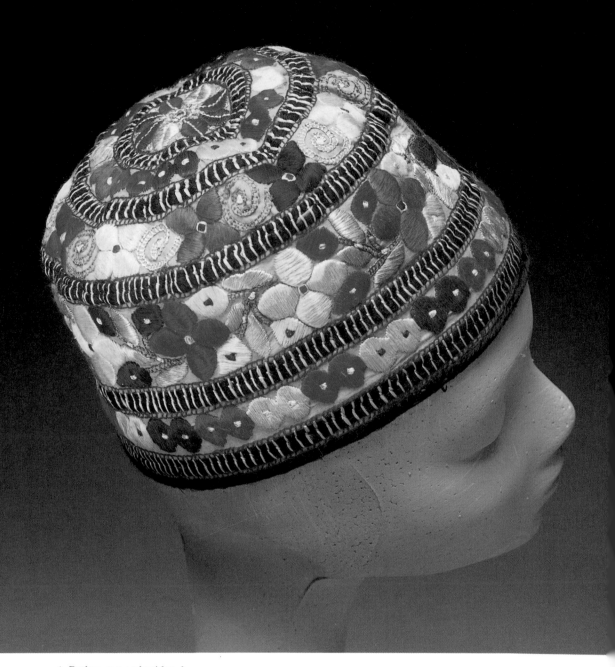

4. Pathan cap embroidered
in silk floss on yellow cotton
in satin stitch panels
separated by bands couched
with Oriental stitch. North
West India, mid twentieth
century

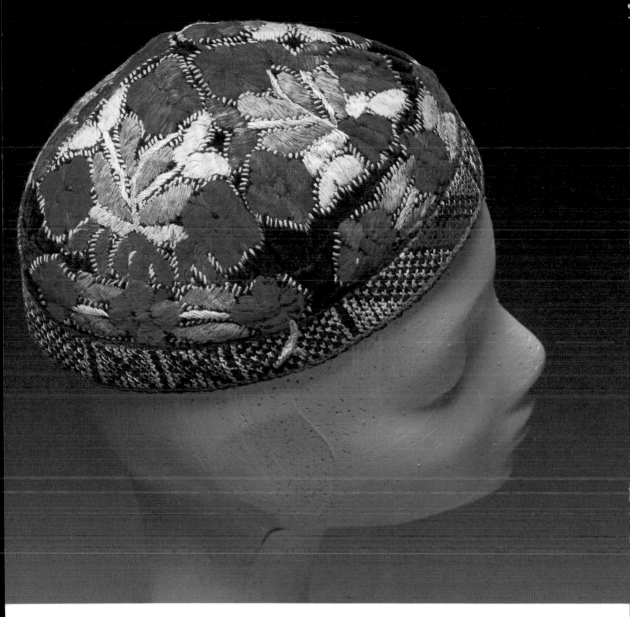

5. Pathan cap embroidered
with silk floss in satin stitch
and stroke stitch on black
velvet. The cap is finished
with a band of cross stitch
worked over a strip of black
cotton knitting. India, mid
twentieth century

57

The rough glass mirrors, which are firmly attached to the background fabric before the surrounding embroidery is worked, are a very powerful protection from evil, as any spirit seeing its reflection in one of the mirrors would be terrified and flee. *Shishadur* is widespread throughout India, Pakistan, and Afghanistan, and the accompanying embroidery varies from the severely geometrical in the north, to the free work of Sind on the Indian Ocean. In the past it was worked with silk floss hand-woven cotton, or silk (Figs 47, 48).

Two other very distinct Indian embroidery styles are *Phulkari* and *Chikankari*. *Phulkari*, which is an embroidery of the Punjab, is so unlike any other embroidery found in India that it is thought to predate the Moghul influence. Some of the earliest pieces were, with their repeated spot motifs, remarkably like damask weaving, and so may have been embroidery deliberately imitating weaving. The embroidery is worked from the back using silk floss. As virtually the whole fabric is covered with thread, these pieces are very time-consuming to darn, and this makes their export potential limited. They therefore tend to be worked as family heirlooms (Fig 28).

Chikankari from Lucknow, Dacca and the Ganges plain is the only white-work done in India apart from some tambouring on muslin, and some imitation Ayrshire work. Although there are references to some *chikankari* being worked on off-white tussore silk, it is better known as white embroidered muslin. The name *chikan* seems to cover everything from white shadow work to pulled fillings, and the special seed stitches, all of which are worked on gossamer fine muslin in two

FIG 46 Detail from an ari of an elephant, worked in chain stitch in twisted silk thread on cotton ground. India, second half twentieth century

FIG 47 Detail from a *chakla* patched from worn-out clothing, *shisha* glass, couching and geometrical satin stitch. North-west India, second half twentieth century

FIG 48 Detail from a skirt in the style of Sindi embroidery. Navy-blue cotton fabric 14 threads/cm (35 threads/in). Embroidered with three strands of stranded cotton in mid green, pink, purple, in geometrical satin stitch, cross stitch, shisha stitch and single Oriental stitch. India, modern

59

FIG 49 Detail from a cloth in Chikan work. Embroidered in two weights of cotton thread on very fine muslin in buttonhole stitch, back stitch, Phanda knot, Murri stitch, Chikan stem stitch, in a tree of life pattern made up of *buti*. Ganges Plains, mid twentieth century

weights of thread. The main thread is like coton-á-broder, and quite heavy on the delicate fabric, while the pulled fillings are worked in a fine sewing thread. The origin of the work is not known, although one theory has it being introduced into India by Muslims trading with the Far East. What is known is that it was a flourishing industry at the end of the nineteenth century, worked both as a cottage industry and by professional Muslim embroiderers. Apart from *chikankari*, Indian embroidery is extremely colourful, with reds predominating, following by a riot of yellow, greens, purple, and orange.

The motifs of Indian embroidery are a mixture of Hindu gods, peacocks, the sun, eight-pointed stars, parakeets, flowers from western influences, and the *buta* and tree of life from Persia. There is no attempt at realism, figures being portrayed in primitive fashion. Some designs are strictly geometrical, covering the entire fabric, while others are arranged as spot motifs surrounded by several borders.

5 | Palestine

The embroidery of Palestine comes from a very small, but historically famous, area. Unfortunately, as little, if any, survives from before the end of the nineteenth century; everything illustrated here belongs to the twentieth century. Although most of the embroidery that has survived is the work of *fellahin* women who lived in villages scattered throughout Galilee, Judea, Samaria and the coastal strip by the Mediterranean, there is also a small amount of semi-professional work from the area around Bethlehem. In contrast to the couched cords and gold threads of the Bethlehem embroiderers, the *fellahin* embroidery was worked mainly in cross stitch.

Palestine has been fought over since the dawn of history. The earliest inhabitants are thought to have been Canaanites who migrated from the Arabian peninsula. Invasions of the country by Hebrews, Persians, Greeks, Romans, Crusaders, and Ottoman Turks followed over the centuries; the Ottoman rule lasted over 400 years, ending only with the British Mandate in the early twentieth century. Despite all the political upheavals, it is surprising how little impact these outside influences had on the native embroidery. The Bethlehem embroiderers owe something to the styles of Greece, Turkey and Persia, but the old, severely geometrical cross stitch patterns belong to the eastern Mediterranean tradition. In 1948 Palestine as a country ceased to exist when it was partitioned into Isreal and Jordan, but the people of Palestine, fearful of losing their identity, are today reviving their old crafts and again embroidering their ancient motifs.

The earliest textile fibres associated with Palestine were cotton and flax. As early as 480 BC it was recorded that cotton was being cultivated in Judea and that the fibres there were yellower than those of the cotton plants growing in Egypt. Spinning and weaving were certainly practised in Palestine from ancient times. As well as cotton and flax, animal wool and hair were gathered for spinning, and eventually, when silkworms were smuggled out of China, there was a silk industry. Originally, almost all the embroidery was counted work on homespun hand-woven cotton or linen fabric. Strangely enough, perhaps the greatest external influence was that of machine-made textiles. During the British Mandate, these became more readily available. This posed an enormous problem, as the cotton satins and other finely-woven fabrics were not suitable for counting, while

FIG 50 Jerusalem sampler in red and black on Ramallah cloth. This is a closely woven double weave that is easy to count. Patterns include talisman, cypress trees, the leach, squared palms and several small borders (Figs 88a, f, g, 93c, d, e, 100a, b, e). Mid twentieth century

FIG 51 Detail from a cloth in two shades of green on Ramallah cloth. Worked in cross stitch. The patterns include a border of the tree of the big half opened bud, wider border with flower pot shows western influence and a solid panel of chevron palm leaves joined together and typical of Ramallah dress back panels. Palestine, modern

almost all the traditional patterns were counted. To overcome this, when working the old patterns specially woven cloth, or sometimes canvas, is attached to the area to be embroidered. When the embroidery is finished, the open-woven cloth or canvas threads are removed one by one.

The colour most common in Palestinian clothing was dark blue, although black was also worn, and around Ramallah, white. As well as the gold, silver, and silk cords of Bethlehem work, silk floss was also used for embroidery. Almost all the silk floss used was dark red, although small amounts of cerise, purple, green, orange and black can be found. Recently, the silk floss has been replaced by mercerised cotton and pearl thread, but the colours remain much the same. The early embroideries all have a heavy, overstuffed look, the background material being completely covered with thread. Of the few stitches used in Palestinian embroidery, the most common is cross stitch, which is worked in various geometrical patterns. The Bethlehem embroiderers used couching to hold down their heavy threads, and a small amount of satin stitch for special fillings.

The motifs in Palestinian embroidery are all named, although the names used vary from place to place. It is always debatable whether the motif came first, and suggested the name, or there was a deliberate attempt to design a motif to represent a flower, tree, or some other object. The motifs range from rosettes to cypress and palm trees, talismans, flower pots, and birds (Figs 50, 51, 52). Because to travel any distance was difficult before the days of good roads and motor transport, there was little contact with the world beyond the

6. Chest panel worked in Fibrone, an early wood pulp yarn imitating silk floss on black handwoven cotton in cross stitch. In Arab dress the chest panel is most important. The head, neck and chest areas were thought to be the main life centres of the body and needed protection against evil spirits. This protection was given by beads, talismans and embroidery. In this panel the talisman symbol has been embroidered and hangs from the necklace. For some reason the embroidery was never made up into a dress and the neck opening remains uncut. Palestine, Southeast Coastal Plain. 1920.

7. Chest panel of a Bethlehem royal wedding dress. The whole chest panel is called the 'flower pot', and is embroidered before being sewn to the dress. The embroidery of Bethlehem differs from that of the rest of Palestine. Instead of cross stitch it is made up of free flowing borders, separated by bands of silk floss stitches. The borders are made up of couched gilt and silk cords and are more reminiscent of Turkish embroidery than Palestinian. Palestine, 1910

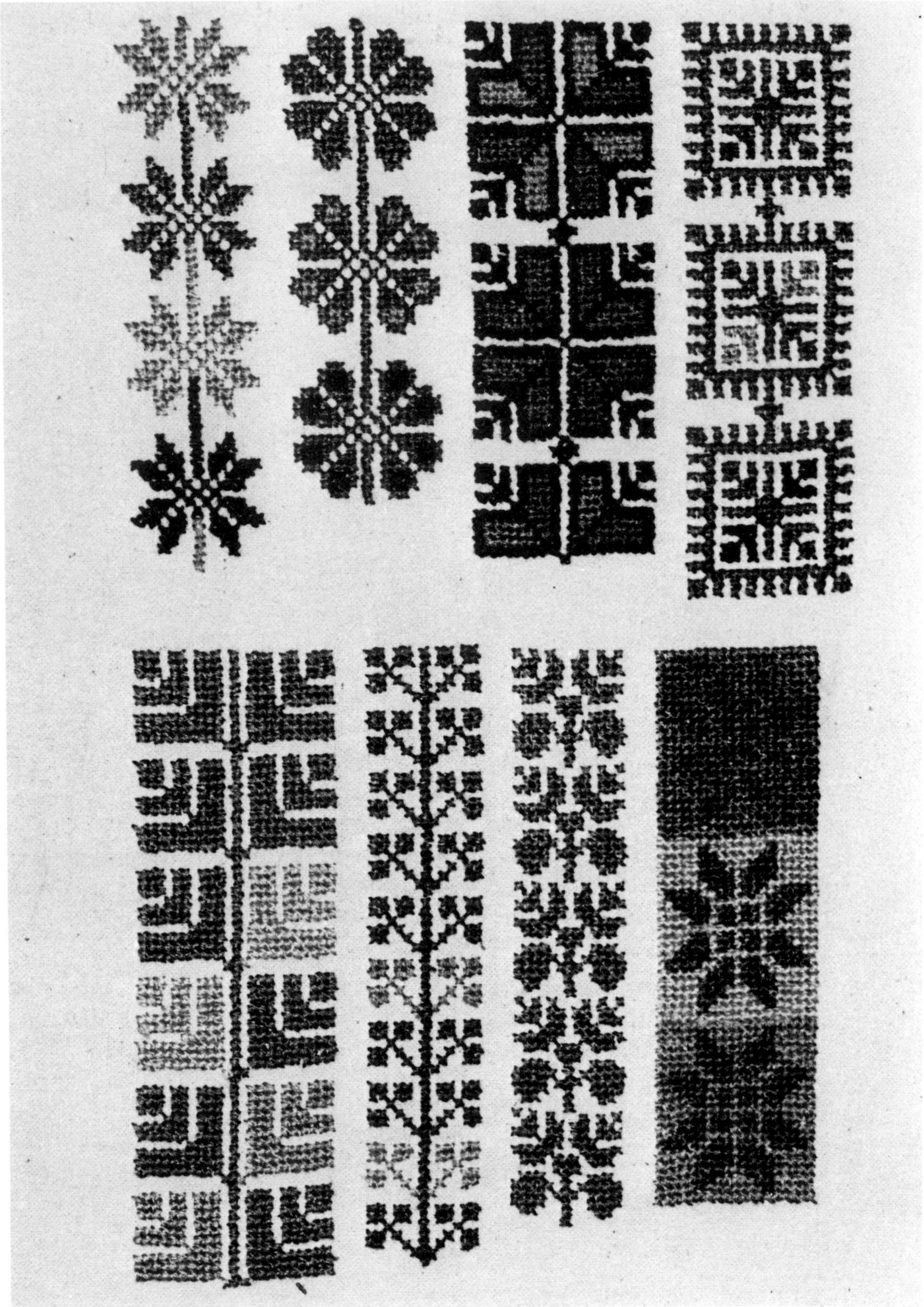

FIG 52 Working sampler on calico of some common patterns. Top row from left: tree of eight; stemmed rosette; squared palm-leaf, the road to Egypt; quatrefoil, officer's badge. Bottom from left; upward growth in squared palm-leaf and small branched stem; floral pattern with probable European influence; eight-pointed star. There is always some uncertainty in naming patterns as the names vary in different parts of the country

FIG 53 Chest panel from a 1950 Palestinian dress. The panel is made up of four border patterns, three main borders and a lesser border repeated four times (Figs 27a, 90a, c, d). Each border has a red background with small amounts of purple, yellow, white, green, blue, gold and pink. It is worked in cross stitch on black sateen

neighbouring villages, and the patterns changed very little, although the arrangement of the motifs varied according to the whim of the embroiderer. The designs that resulted were made up from quite a small collection of patterns; the chest panel (Fig 53) is built up around four patterns, and the back panel uses seven.

Most of the designs come under the heading of border patterns, and while some are balanced four ways (quatrefoil form), and may be worked in any direction, many representing plant forms, symbolising growth, have an upward direction (Fig 54). The Bethlehem chest panel which is called the 'flower pot' is built up in much the same way as the cross-stitched chest panel. The main area is surrounded by narrower and wider borders, each filled with a particular flowing pattern, worked in couching or overcasting. Embroidery was a feature of particular parts of the dress, the chest panel, the back panel, along seams, and on cuffs, but by far the most important area was the chest panel, guarding the most vulnerable part of the body against evil influences.

FIG 54 Detail of a back panel of an indigo blue dress, woven with a pink and fushia stripe. The panel has been roughly sewn to the dress and was originally part of a side panel of a much earlier dress. It is worked in cross stitch in cyclamen and silvery lavender silk floss. The narrow border is one of the most common framing borders (Fig 96a), while the two wider borders are unusual and probably show western influence (Figs 97a, b). Palestine, twentieth century

8. Back panel from a Palestinian dress, 1950. Next in importance to the chest panel was the back panel. It is worked in cross stitch on black sateen. The homewoven cloth has given way to machine-made cloth and the silk floss to pearl cotton, while the main panel has a western influence

6

Yugoslavia

The historical background of Yugoslavia is very muddled. Once part of the Balkans along with Greece, Albania, Bulgaria and Romania, it has been inhabited constantly since the Old Stone Age. At different times it has been dominated by Greece, Rome, Turkey and Austria, and it is only since 1918 that it became the Yugoslavia that we know today.

Although the working of embroidery was fairly widespread through the various states that make up the modern country, these embroideries come from a small area of Dalmatia along the Adriatic coast, with one possibly from Montenegro. They are particularly interesting in that they show techniques and stitches that were once embroidered on clothing. The stitches and designs are almost identical to the early patterns, but with the need to embroider clothing become a thing of the past, they have been retained on table linen. While the appliqués and braiding that went with tailoring were done by men, the cross stitch and pattern darning embroideries were centred on the home.

In rural areas, women were skilled in weaving linen and wool. In some areas they were so skilled at weaving that they preferred to weave patterns into their clothing, and it was only on the collars and front opening bands, the *oshvitza*, (Fig 55) that there was any embroidery. If there was time after the farm work was done, grandmothers, daughters and granddaughters embroidered together. One Yugoslav woman, remembering the afternoons spent embroidering, explained how each worker knew how long it would take her to embroider a particular motif, the area to be worked would be marked out by needle, and the amount of stitching to be done that day planned.

The threads used were originally silk, linen, wool and goats' hair. These were homespun and, in the case of silk and wool, home dyed. In some areas, lavish use was made of bought metallic threads as well. The patterns were mostly counted, although some free work was embroidered in satin stitch, chain stitch, and Romanian stitch, and the gold and silver braids were attached with back stitch or couching. These embroideries have all been worked this century.

The early twentieth century embroideries (Fig 57) all have very strong growth patterns which first appeared on headscarves and

FIG 55 Enlarged detail from the front border of the *oshvita*. These were made up of collars and front opening bands which were embroidered separately. They often supplied the only embroidery on the dress. Worked in cross stitch in red, green, blue and gold, and counted over two threads of 13 threads/cm (33 threads/in) cream cotton. Montenegro, mid twentieth century

9. Buta. Detail from a large bed cover. The large *buta* is filled with flowers and surrounded by borders of smaller *buti* worked in closed herringbone stitch in silk floss on cotton. Herringbone stitch was much used in ethnic embroidery, as it covers the fabric with great economy of thread. Greek Islands

FIG 56 Detail from a cloth
worked in bands of satin
stitch and outlined with
double running. Yugoslavia,
early twentieth century

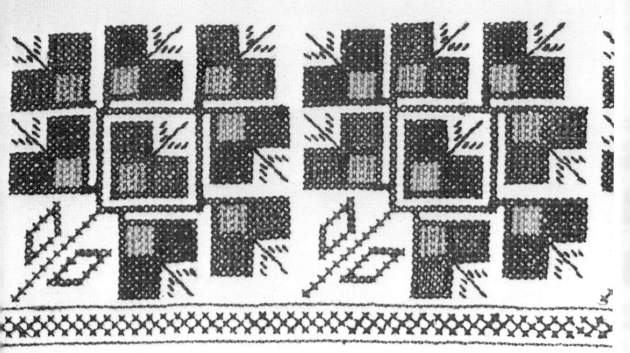

head-shawls. These motifs were placed diagonally in a corner of the scarf and, when worked in cross stitch, were accompanied by long lines of double running and small double running curls that lightened the rather heavy cross-stitch motifs. Another feature of these scarf patterns were spot motifs worked in long rows or sometimes linked by a single double running line. In Fig 80 the spot motifs have been worked on the diagonal, and are a compromise with small running stitches that just fall short of being joined together.

The pattern darning or damask darning examples come from Konavli and, although they are modern, the motifs are from much earlier *oshvitza*. While the front edging borders from Montenegro were narrow, in some central and coastal areas there was also a much wider-fronted type similar to a Palestinian chest panel. This was usually covered with pattern darning or damask darning with satin stitch and slanting Slav stitch. Pattern or damask darning is often thought of as a method of obtaining a woven-type pattern with embroidery when the weaver lacks the necessary expertise to weave the pattern; but these Yugoslav women were expert weavers and it could be that their use of the word damask is the key, and that it was a peasant's way of copying with silk thread and embroidery the richly woven damasks of Turkey and Persia. The embroidery in silk in some cases almost completely covered the linen background and just as the *Phulkari* from India is worked from the back, so too is the pattern darning still worked in Konavli. When the chest panels were attached to the garment, the outer edges were neatened by a row of plait stitch. This was sometimes in gold metallic thread, but more often in gold or yellow silk thread, and several of the modern cloths have retained this row of plait stitch, still in gold coloured thread and now just an unnecessary addition to the pattern darning (Figs 58–61).

FIG 57 Detail from a cloth worked in cross stitch and double running in red, dark blue, grey and yellow on cotton, 12 threads/cm (30 threads/in) showing strong growth pattern. The direction of the cross stitch changes in each centre for greater emphasis. Yugoslavia, early twentieth century

FIG 58 Detail from a cloth worked in damask darning and satin stitch. The darning has been edged with rows of plait stitch. In early chest panels of damask darning from coastal areas, plait stitch was used to neaten the edge and is still retained here, although this is modern work. Konavli, 1980

FIG 59 Enlarged detail from a cloth of damask darning similar to that worked on the wide *oshvitza* from the central and coastal areas. Konavli, 1980

74

FIG 60 Detail from a cloth of
rayed motifs similar to those
used to form a border at the
edge of the wide *oshvitza* of
the central and coastal
areas. Konavli, 1980

FIG 61 Detail from a cloth,
damask darning and satin
stitch on white fabric, 10
threads/cm (24 threads/in)
in stranded cotton in red,
dark blue, dark green, gold.
Konavli, 1980

7

From rose
to carnation

A motif that appears in early woven textiles, (especially those from
the Mediterranean area), in Palestinian embroidery and throughout
Europe in cross stitch embroidery is that of the so-called rosette or
rose. It is called by many different names, but it is basically a very
simple geometrical design, commonly built within a 15 x 15 unit
square. At first glance, this would appear to be a rather limiting space
in which to arrange an interesting pattern, but this is not the case, and
the seemingly primitive design lends itself to many variations. The
rosette often appears in the design form of Fig 62a, but in Fig 62b
showing a detail from the back panel of a 1950 Palestinian dress, the
veins and spaces between the 'petals' are stitched in a contrasting
colour for each unit of four flowers, radically altering the design.
While the basic shape is kept the same, the 'petals' can be lightened by
omitting four stitches (Fig 62c), or changed by the addition of a
contrasting colour, commonly orange, black and dark blue within the
red 'petal' (Fig 62d). The motif can be further altered by changing and
enlarging the centre while at the same time reducing the 'petal' area
(Fig 62e), or by making the outline more toothed so that it now
resembles a carnation (Figs 62f, g). Still working within the framework of the 15-unit square, other, more complicated designs can be
made (Figs 62i, j, k, l).

The rose motif in Palestinian embroidery is arranged in well defined
ways. It can be used in a single vertical column, as a double row, or as
an overall pattern (Fig 63). It is usually surrounded by a frame (Fig
64), which is so arranged that in the overall pattern, it makes a new
pattern within the pattern. All the variations of the rosette either fit
within this frame or that of Fig 65. To clear the slightly larger corner,
the frame needs to be enlarged by two squares and altered slightly
(Fig 65).

FIG 62 The transition of the
rose design to that of the
carnation

78

a

b

c

d

e

f

g

h

i

j

k

l

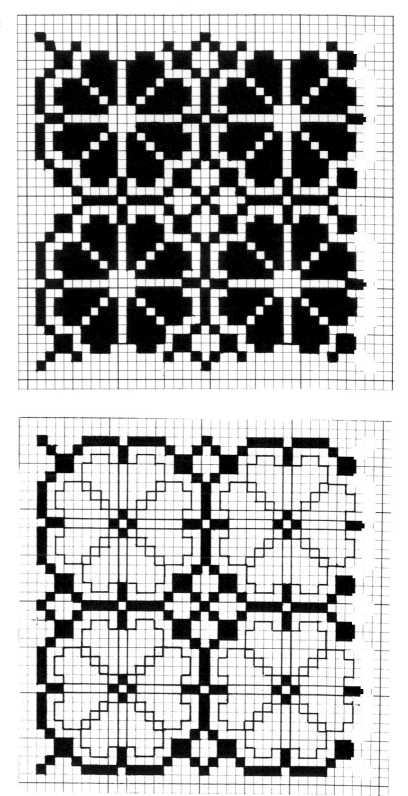

FIG 63 Overall pattern built
up from rosette

FIG 64 Framing pattern
within the pattern

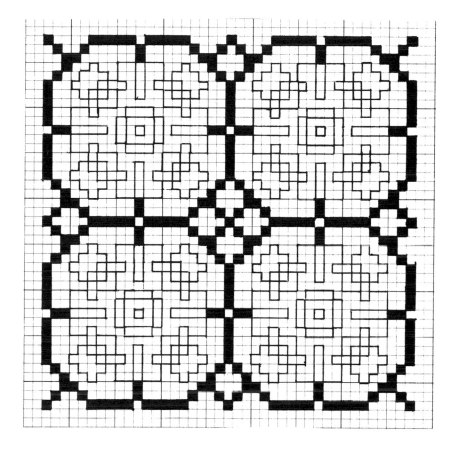

FIG 65 Larger framing pattern for Fig 62

8

Peacocks, pomegranates and more carnations

Throughout history, certain motifs keep appearing, carved in stone or wood, painted on ceramics and woven into or printed on textiles. There is considerable borrowing from one medium by another, so it is not really surprising that the same motifs also feature in embroidery design. The original symbolism of the motif is often long forgotten or, at best, only partly understood. This is especially so when the design has been taken over and adapted by a totally different culture, as is the case with the Persian motif that became the basis of the Paisley shawl design; yet it still persists. One such is the peacock motif from Indian and Persian versions of the tree of life.

Of all the motifs found in ethnic embroidery, the tree of life, in all its many forms and interpretations, must be the most universal. One of the earliest records of it is carved into stone from Assyria in the ninth century BC, and depicts a stylised date palm flanked by two attendant figures, with human bodies but heads and wings of eagles, fertilising the tree (Fig 66). Over the years the attendants became animals, sometimes birds, and in India, the attendant becomes a peacock (Figs 67, 68). The tree, which had been venerated from much earlier times as the almost divine producer of food, drink and shelter, changed with the years, and by early Christian times had become either a chalice, a pedestal or a column.

FIG 66 Assyrian tree of life

FIG 67 Detail from an ari of
a peacock, silk thread on
brown cotton in chain
stitch. India, second half
twentieth century

FIG 68 Enlarged detail of
one of the classical
representations of the
peacock. Kathiawar, Persia

The peacock had been regarded as sacred in ancient Rome because
it was believed that its flesh was incorruptible, and it soon became a
symbol of immortality. Adopted by the early Christians, it came to
also symbolise the resurrection. With its now Christian connections,
it spread to the ethnic embroideries of Europe either as part of the tree
of life motif, or sometimes without the tree, as a running border. The
tree of life theme was retained in many Assisi embroidery patterns
(Fig 69) while in India and Morocco a form of the tree was retained
without the attendants (Figs 70–72). The origins of the tree of life
were more eastern than western, and over a period of time a new
version appeared. The tree became planted in the chalice of the
western world, and became further transformed into the herb pots of
countless samplers. Meanwhile Persian textiles and carpets displayed
vases of flowers symmetrically arranged with small attendant birds
hovering about the flowers.

83

FIG 69 Tree of life with peacocks retained in Assisi work. Cross stitch and double running

FIG 70 Detail from ari of tree of life motif. There are peacocks in the same ari but they have moved from beside the tree and are now spot motifs. India

FIG 72 Detail from a
Moroccan bolster of a row of
tree life motifs, worked on
unbleached cotton, in heavy
silk thread in red, burgundy,
green, light and dark blue,
over four threads in cross
stitch and plait stitch

FIG 71 Detail from modern
Sindi embroidery of the tree
of life, worked on navy-blue
cotton in mid green, dark
pink, and mauve with some
shisha glass

87

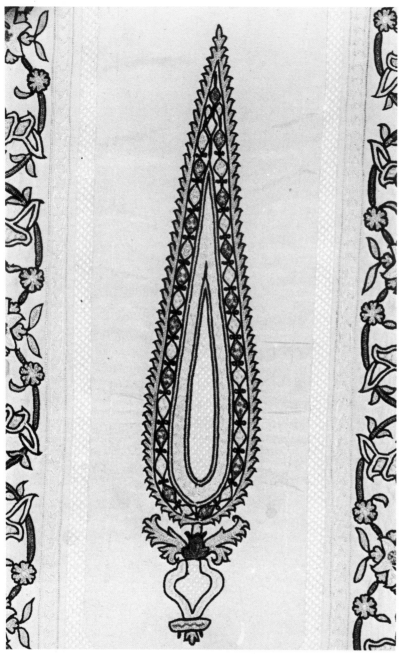

FIG 73 Detail from a cloth, cypress tree worked in twisted silk thread in chain stitch. Persia, early twentieth century

Cypress trees

Tall, slender cypress trees (Fig 73) have always featured in Persian textile and embroidery designs, but alongside these trees another tree-like motif appears that is even more famous. It appears in many Caucasian and Persian carpets, in Indian embroideries from Kashmir, in Indian cotton textiles and on every Paisley shawl. Variations of this motif are so widespread that it goes by many names; *buta, boteh*, pine cone, seed, leaf, pear, mango, almond and paisley. Sometimes it

FIG 74 Detail from a cloth, row of cypress trees in cross stitch on black cotton in red, pink, yellow, blue, green and purple, counted over three threads

88

FIG 75 *Buta* still looking like a cypress tree from a raw silk jacket embroidered in silk floss. Kashmir

FIG 76 *Buta*, looking more like a paisley motif

FIG 77 *Buta* shape filled with flowers, the outline gone

FIG 78 Detail from a cashmere shawl of a *buta* embroidered in silk floss in outline stitch and Oriental stitch. Kashmir, mid twentieth century

FIG 79 Detail from a Greek Island bed cover of a *buta*, worked silk floss on cotton in closed herringbone stitch. Late nineteenth century

is made up of an outline filled with a collection of flowers and leaves (colour photo 9), sometimes the outline moves to the centre with the flowers and leaves on the outside (Fig 76), and sometimes the motif just takes the classic shape without any outline (Fig 77). The variations are endless and its origin unknown; perhaps it is nothing more than a tall tree pointing to the heavens and bending to the wind.

The pomegranate

Another motif that appears frequently in both free and counted ethnic embroidery is the pomegranate. Originally a native of Persia and Afghanistan, it has been cultivated for hundreds of years and is now established in all countries bordering the Mediterranean. Because of its many seeds, Greek myth associated the pomegranate with fertility, yet it always carried the underlying association with death. When Pluto carried off Persephone to the underworld, her grieving mother, the goddess of the corn, vowed there would be no harvest. Zeus commanded Pluto to return Persephone to earth, but before he did so he gave her a pomegranate seed to eat, ensuring that she would return to him every year. Persephone was the corn maiden, the symbol of the new corn and this neatly tied the pomegranate to a much older fertility cult, practised since man first planted grain for ensuring a good harvest. The pomegranate was to become much more acceptable to the early church than the cult of the corn maiden. Perhaps the frequency with which the pomegranate appeared stitched on funeral sheets is not so surprising after all.

By 126 BC, the pomegranate had reached China where it became a Buddhist sign – the essence of the favourable influence – the hope that

FIG 80 Detail from cloth of pomegranates, embroidered in cross stitch on cotton in red, gold, green, blue, grey and brown, over two threads. Material 12 threads/cm (30 threads/in) Yugoslavia, mid twentieth century

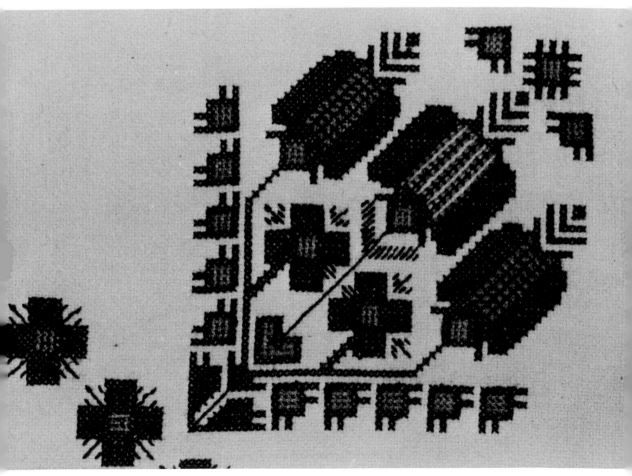

the family would have many respectful and virtuous children who would bring them credit and fame. The large, beautifully-shaped fruit which ripens to a rich maroon colour and eventually splits open to reveal numerous seeds, is surmounted by a little crown that figures predominately in all pomegranate designs. The fruit has always been a symbol of fertility and, not without a little cynicism, the symbol of democracy; the valuble part being the many seeds surmounted by the worthless crown.

Carnation

The carnation is one of the most common flowers to be found in ethnic embroidery, either worked in a type of feather stitch, peculiar to the island of Crete, or as cross stitch and plait stitch in embroideries from the Greek islands and throughout Europe. It belongs to the Dianthus family, first recorded and named dianthus or 'divine flower' in the fourth century BC and native to Europe, Asia, and parts of North Africa.

Its history is very muddled, as it has been grown and cross-bred for hundreds of years. Before 1500 it appears to have been lumped together with gillyflowers in an assortment of spellings. When it finally appeared in its own right, there was great confusion as to whether it was a 'coronation' or a 'carnation'. 'Coronation' suggested that it was dented and toothed above like a little coronet; 'carnation' came from the word 'incarnation', meaning it was a light rosy pink or flesh-colour. Although 'coronation' is thought by some to be the original name, after 1600 this word went out of use and it became a carnation. The 'coronation' or toothedness of the petals which had been its distinguishing mark in all embroidery designs was to some extent lost when a smooth, unfringed petal was developed in some varieties in the eighteenth century. Rather than being loaded with symbolism, the carnation just appears to have been a much-loved flower.

9

Techniques

The graphs and line drawings

The graphs have been presented as such for a reason. In graphs with many small symbols it is often hard to see the rhythm in the pattern. Many patterns in ethnic embroidery are in one colour; in others one colour predominates. Where there are several colours, there is always a dominant theme running throughout the pattern, and you need to see this movement without clutter. In each case the predominant colour is shown in solid black, as is the pattern movement. The line drawings are all shown actual size. Counted patterns can be enlarged or reduced by your choice of background material.

If it is not possible to count the fabric, canvas can be tacked over the area to be worked, and Fig 81 shows five sizes of canvas worked with the appropriate thread. Free patterns can be enlarged or reduced by the graph method. This is given in every embroidery text, but it is time-consuming and not always satisfactory; it is preferable to step into the twentieth century and make use of one of the many copying machines that enlarge and reduce. The time you have saved will be much better spent learning the complex nature and limitations of some of the special stitches. The patterns range from the sophistication of the *buta* to the naïveté of the peacock motifs, but even in the most naïve of the peacocks, the essence has been captured with understatement and often with a fleeting humour.

FIG 81 Enlarging and reducing counted patterns. Counted patterns may be enlarged by counting them over a fabric with fewer threads to the inch. The smaller the thread count, the larger the pattern. Conversely, the greater the thread count, the smaller the pattern will be. The same rules apply when working over canvas attached to fine material. The photos show five grades of double mesh canvas:
a) 4 double threads/cm (10 double threads/in);
b) 5 double threads/cm (12 double threads/in)
c) 6 double threads/cm (15 double threads/in);
d) 7 double threads/cm (18 double threads/in);
e) 8 double threads/cm (21 double threads/in).
It is important to vary the weight of thread to cover the canvas:
4/cm (10/in) 4 ply tapestry wool
5/cm (12/in) 2 strands crewel wool
6/cm (15/in) 3 strands stranded cotton
7/cm (18/in) 2 strands stranded cotton
8/cm (21/in) 2 strands stranded cotton

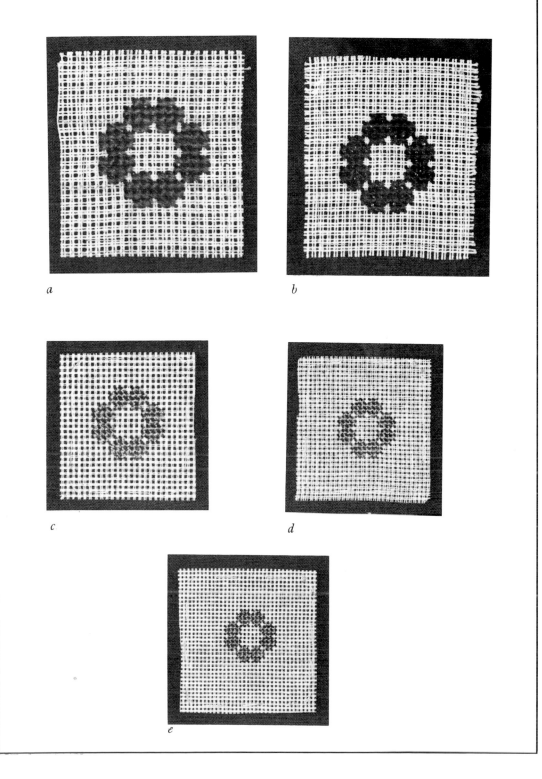

a

b

c

d

e

a

b

c

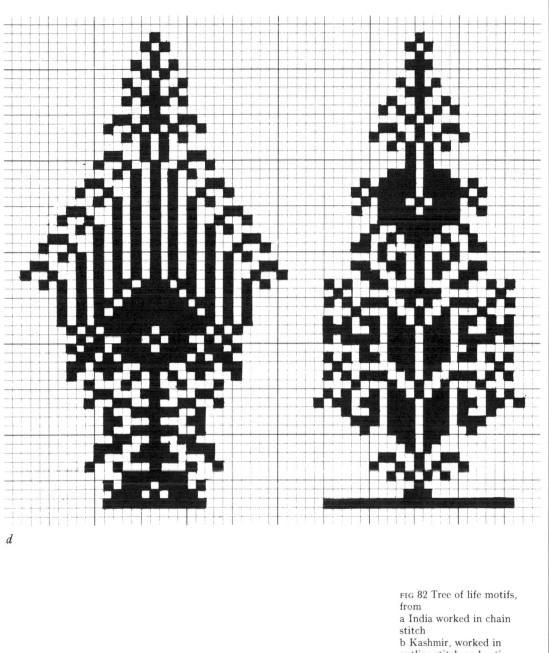

d

FIG 82 Tree of life motifs,
from
a India worked in chain
stitch
b Kashmir, worked in
outline stitch and satin
stitch
c Ganges plains, worked in
Chikan stitches
d Morocco, worked in cross
stitch and plait stitch

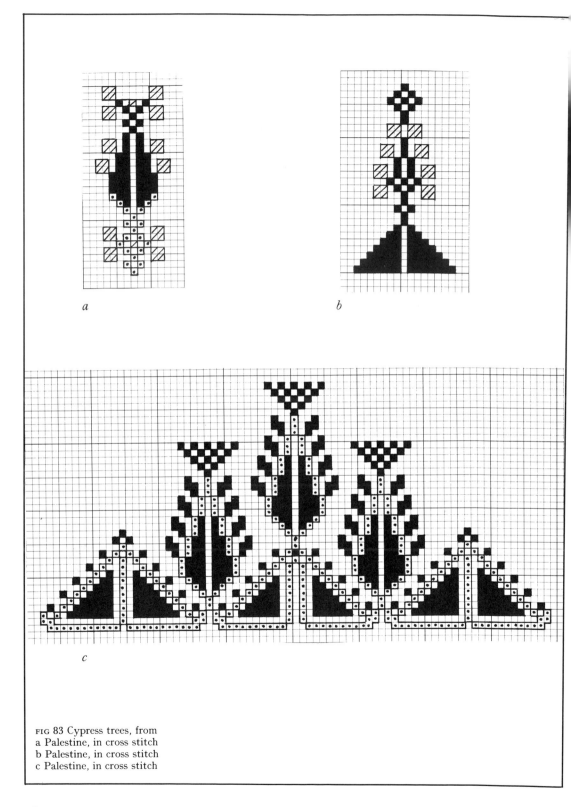

FIG 83 Cypress trees, from
a Palestine, in cross stitch
b Palestine, in cross stitch
c Palestine, in cross stitch

a

b

FIG 84 *Buta*, from Greek
Islands, in closed
herringbone stitch

FIG 85 Peacocks, from
a Denmark, in cross stitch
b Scotland, in cross stitch
c Denmark, in cross stitch
d Holland, in cross stitch
e India, in chain stitch
f India, in long split stitch
and outline stitch. Circles on
tail in blue, orange, yellow,
green, pink, cream,
cyclamen
g India, in chain stitch
h India, in outline stitch
and satin stitch
i Hungary, in outline stitch,
satin stitch

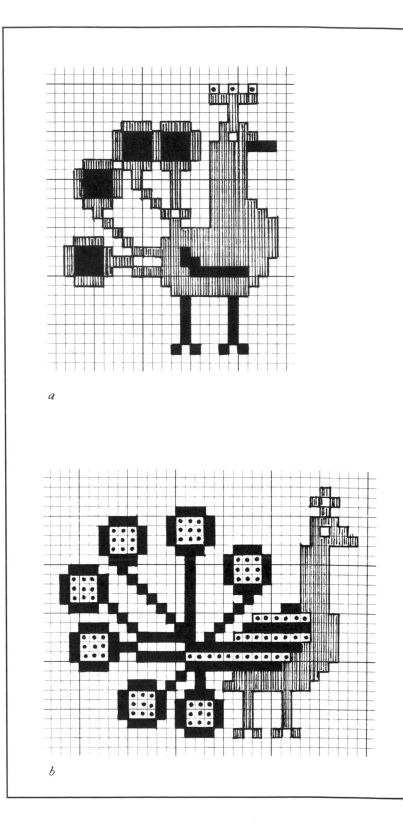

a

b

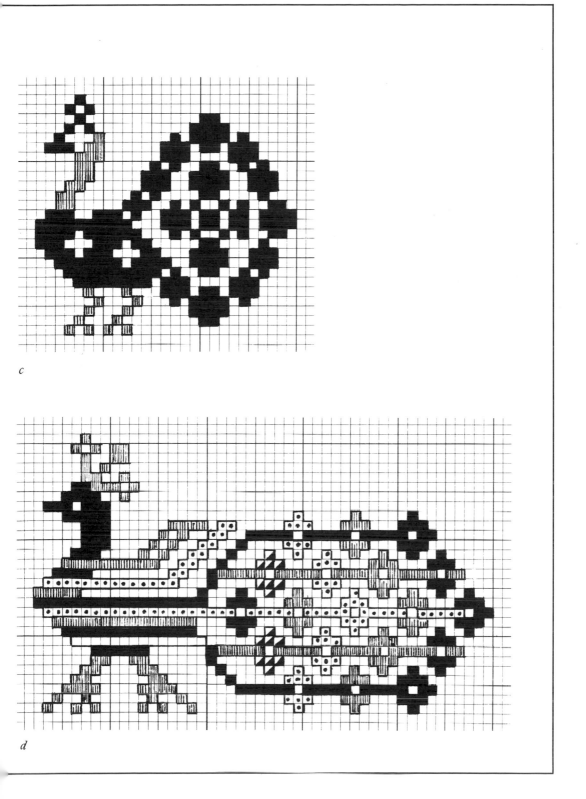

c

d

e

f

g

h

i

a

b

c

d

e

FIG 86 Pomegranates, from
a Switzerland, in outline
stitch and satin stitch
b China, in long-tailed
Chinese knots
c China, in cross stitch
d Yugoslavia, in cross stitch
e Yugoslavia, in cross stitch

f Yugoslavia, in cross stitch
Overleaf
g Europe, in cross stitch
h Bosnia, in cross stitch
i Europe, in cross stitch
j Germany, in cross stitch
k Mexico, in cross stitch

∫

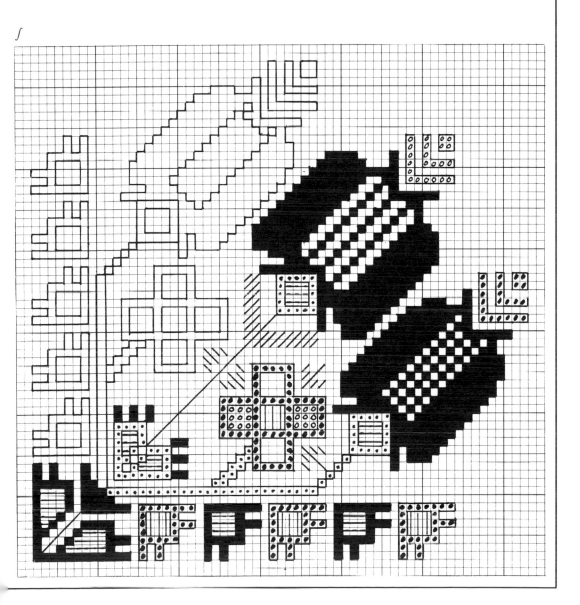

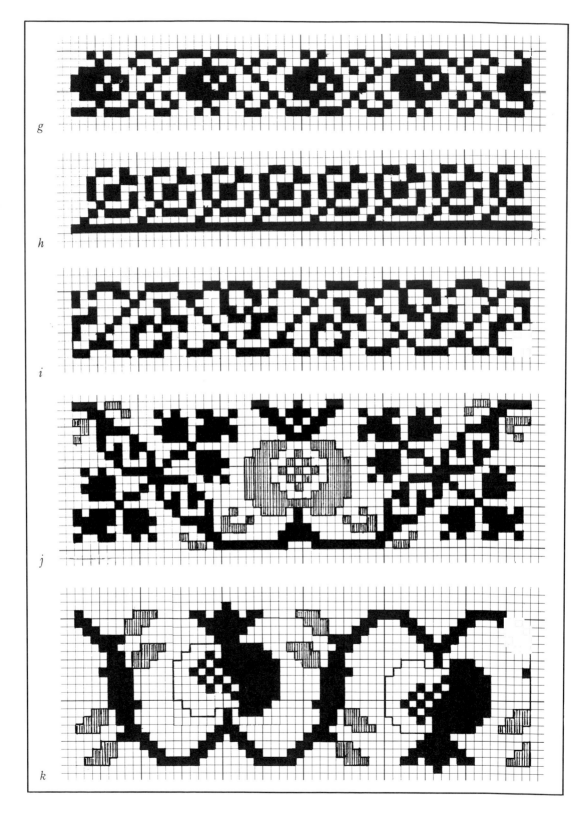

g

h

i

j

k

FIG 87 Carnations, from
a Russia, in cross stitch
b Greek Islands, in red and
green cross stitch
c England, in cross stitch
d Mexico, in cross stitch
e Europe, in cross stitch
f Mexico, in cross stitch
g Greek Islands, in plait
stitch
Overleaf
h Mexico, in cross stitch
i Spain, in green and pink
satin stitch
j England, in cross stitch
and double running
k Germany, in cross stitch
and double running
l Mexico, in cross stitch
m England, in cross stitch
n England, in cross stitch

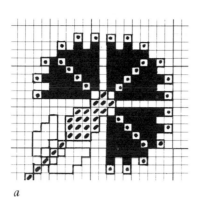

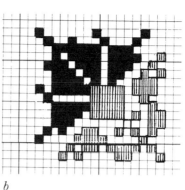

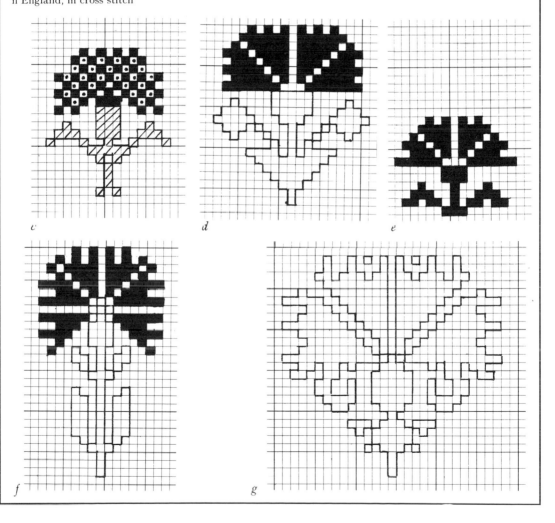

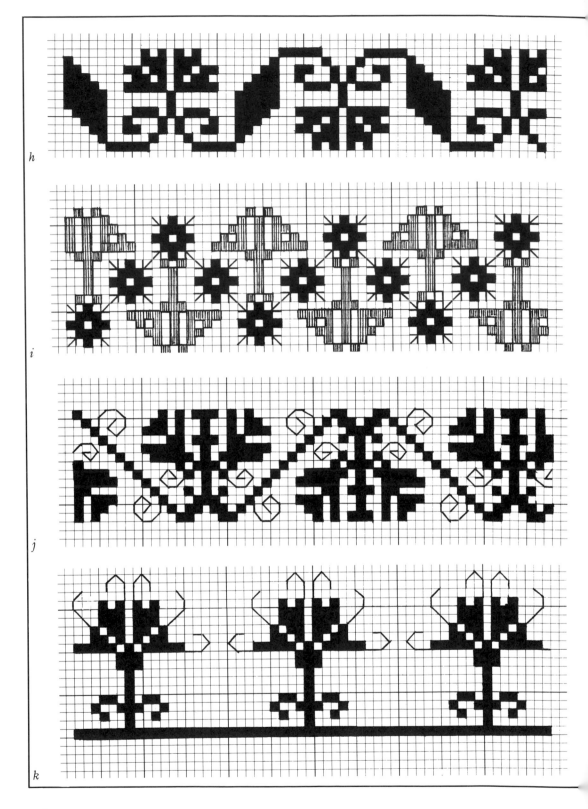

h

i

j

k

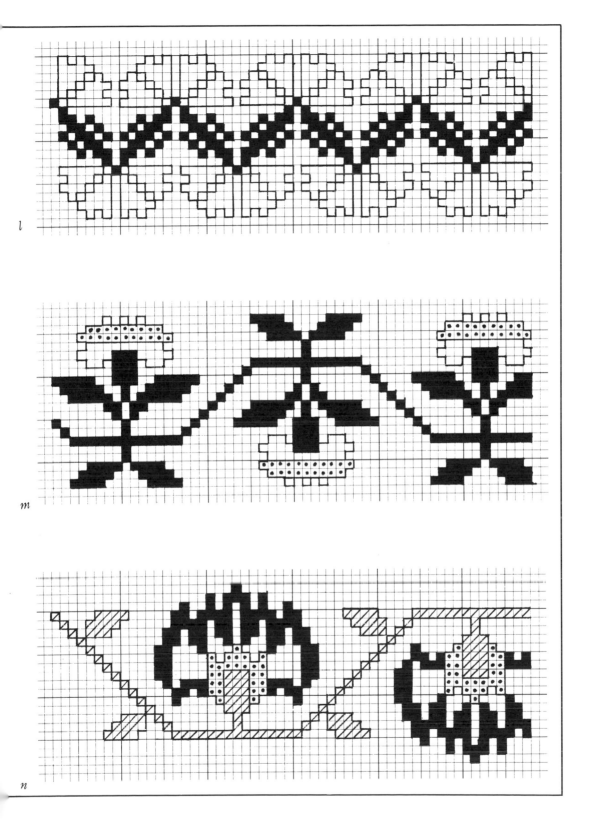

l

m

n

Borders

Another feature of ethnic embroidery design is the border. Just as chest panels, talismans and mirrors served a useful purpose in protecting the wearer from evil influences, so a border was also thought to offer magical protection. It could take any form from a line to a complicated pattern in its own right, often completely out of context with the design theme of the article.

This idea of guarding goes back into antiquity. The earliest known carpet is made up of a field surrounded by ten borders, the five main borders being each guarded by lesser borders. Borders abound on early stone and wood carvings, painted on Egyptian and Assyrian tomb walls and ceramics. One of the borders on the ari (Figs 89a, b) is so nearly identical to an Egyptian border of lotus and buds it seems to have hardly changed on the long journey to India by way of Rome, China and Persia. In Persian carpet design and Indian embroideries made up of spot motifs, the pattern was a continuous design and the border served the purpose of limiting our field of vision, as well as guarding the field. Sometimes the motifs in the field strayed and became part of the border, leaving the field empty. Some embroideries are made up entirely of borders. The Palestinian chest panel (Fig 53) is made up of four main borders which are in turn guarded by a lesser border. In the Moroccan borders (Fig 91) the lesser border (Fig 91a) has become so much a part of the larger border (Figs 91c, d) that it comes as a surprise to realise that it is an addition.

FIG 88 Small borders, from
a Jerusalem sampler, in
cross stitch
b Palestine, in cross stitch
c Chest panel, in cross stitch
d Chest panel, in cross stitch
e *Oshvita,* Montenegro, in
cross stitch
f Palestine, in cross stitch
g Jerusalem sampler, in
cross stitch
h Palestine, in cross stitch
i Palestine, in cross stitch

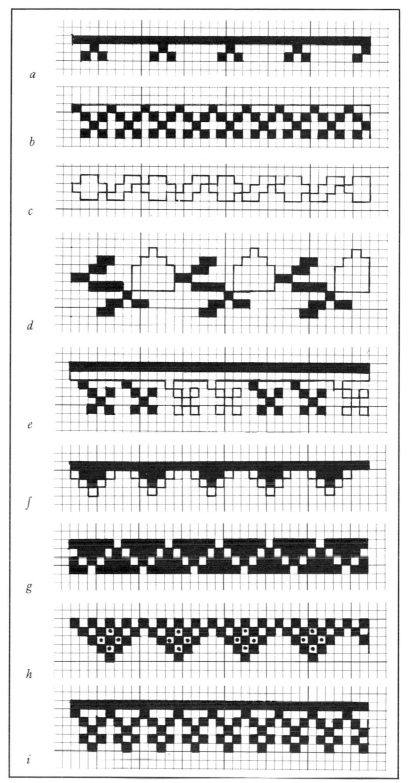

FIG 89a Border of lotus and
cones from Egypt
b Border from ari, India,
4,000 years later

a

b

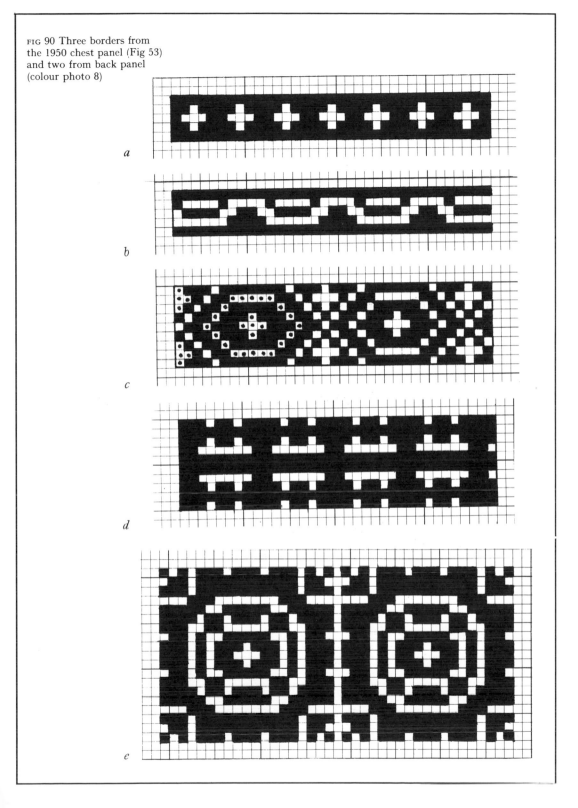

FIG 90 Three borders from the 1950 chest panel (Fig 53) and two from back panel (colour photo 8)

a

b

c

d

e

FIG 91a Small border from Morocco
b Larger border from Morocco, incorporating a small border (Fig 86)
c Larger border from Morocco, incorporating (a)
d Larger border from Morocco, incorporating (a)

a

b

FIG 92 Miscellaneous
patterns from the
embroideries. Animals:
a Elephant from India,
chain stitch
b Lion from India, chain
stitch
Overleaf
c Camel from Egypt, chain
stitch

c

FIG 93 Birds:
a India
b India, chain stitch
c Jerusalem sampler, red
and black cross stitch
d Jerusalem sampler
e Jerusalem sampler

a

b

c

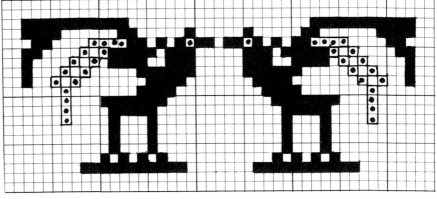

d

e

FIG 94 Flowers:
a Tree peony from China
b Magnolia from China
c Chrysanthemum from
China, satin stitch
d Flower from India, double
running and long split stitch
e Flower from India, chain
stitch
f Flower from India, chain
stitch

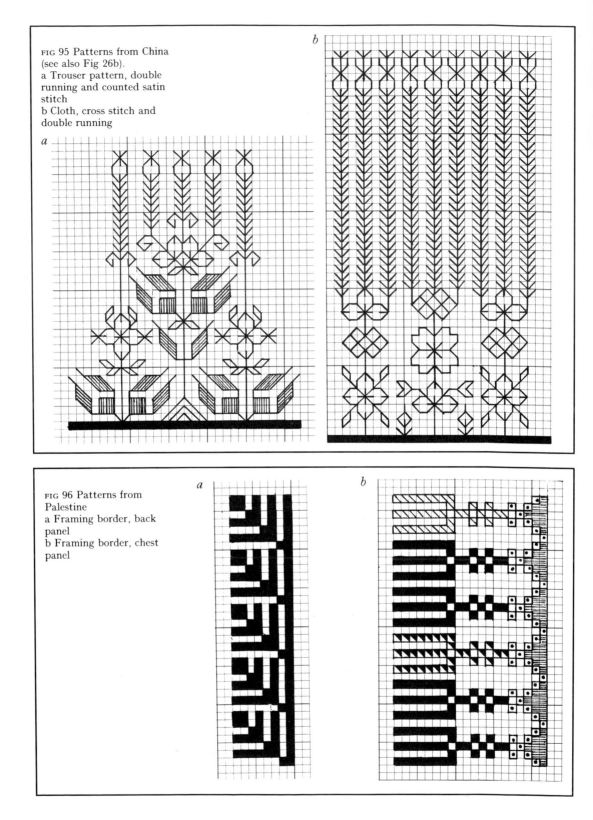

FIG 95 Patterns from China
(see also Fig 26b).
a Trouser pattern, double
running and counted satin
stitch
b Cloth, cross stitch and
double running

FIG 96 Patterns from
Palestine
a Framing border, back
panel
b Framing border, chest
panel

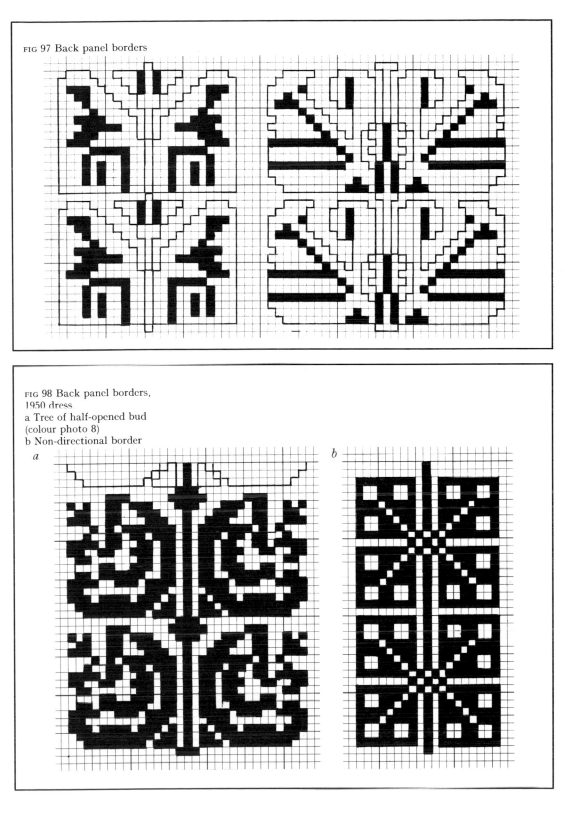

FIG 97 Back panel borders

FIG 98 Back panel borders,
1950 dress
a Tree of half-opened bud
(colour photo 8)
b Non-directional border

a

b

FIG 99 Main back panel

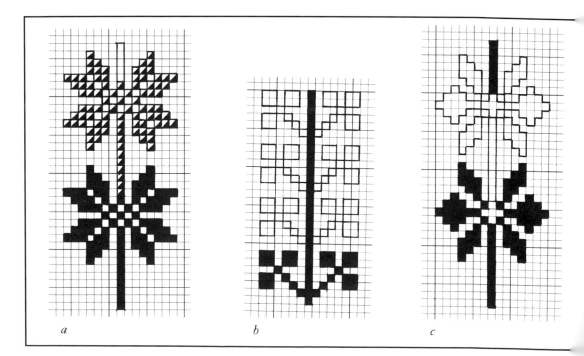

a   b   c

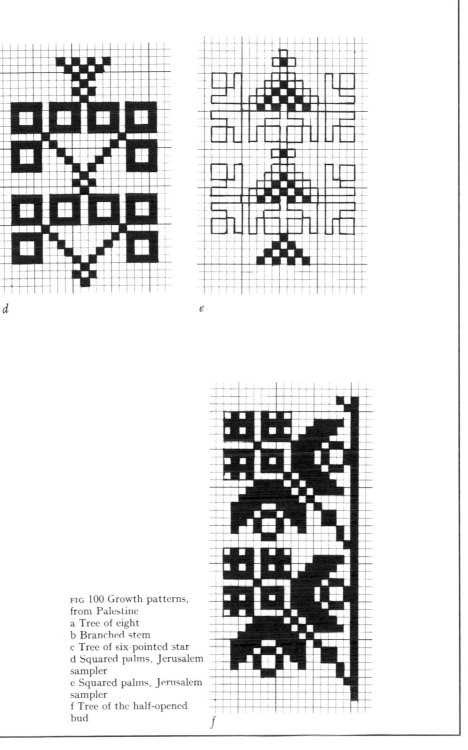

FIG 100 Growth patterns,
from Palestine
a Tree of eight
b Branched stem
c Tree of six-pointed star
d Squared palms, Jerusalem
sampler
e Squared palms, Jerusalem
sampler
f Tree of the half-opened
bud

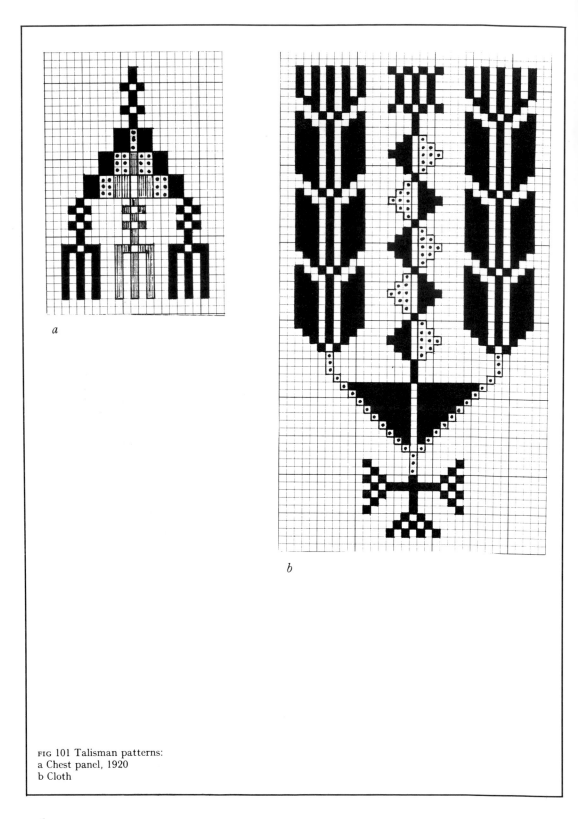

FIG 101 Talisman patterns:
a Chest panel, 1920
b Cloth

a

b

FIG 102 All-over patterns:
a Cloth
b Chest panel, 1920.
Cushions

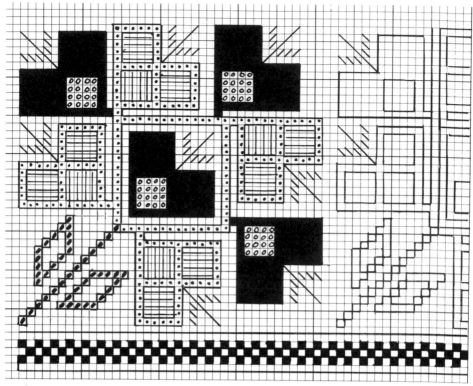

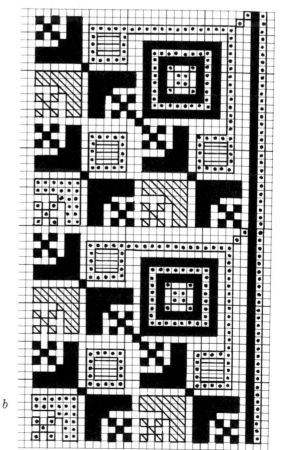

FIG 103 Pattern from
Yugoslavia
a Cross stitch in red, dark
blue, grey and yellow
b *Oshvita* panel, cross stitch
in red, blue, green and
yellow

a

b

128

Counting the uncountable

Although in the past blouses and shirts were made from coarse handwoven linen, nowadays we often prefer to use a finer fabric. Then, the weave was coarse enough to count, but even with a finer fabric it is still possible to use the old traditional counted patterns. This is done by tacking a canvas or evenweave countable material to the finer blouse fabric, embroidering the pattern over the two layers and then withdrawing the canvas threads, one by one. It is important to have the grain of the canvas lying with the grain of the fabric. In many patterns there will be some threads that have not been embroidered over. Remove these first. Then systematically remove

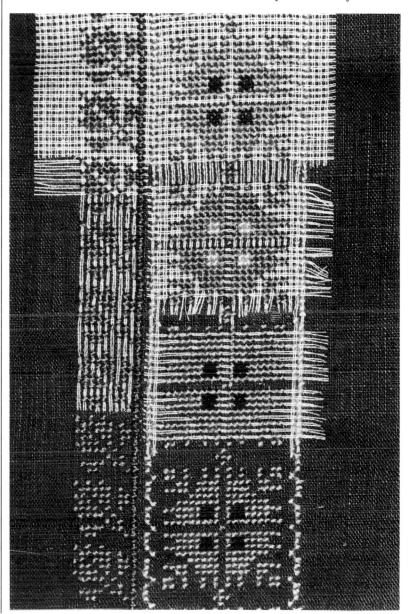

FIG 104 Showing the method of withdrawing the canvas threads from the finished embroidery

129

FIG 105 Blouse pattern
showing the three borders
and the framing border
reversed

all the shorter threads. Finally, withdraw the lengthwise threads. A small pair of tweezers and a little patience are essential.

The scale of the pattern can be altered by using a different count canvas. Before you begin the embroidery, check that your thread is heavy enough to cover the canvas satisfactorily, and to give your work the rich and heavy ethnic look. The embroidered panels measure 25cm x 5cm (10in x 2in) and are made up of three different border patterns. The outside pattern shows strong upward growth and is one of many half-opened bud patterns, while the main pattern is in quatrefoil form and thus nondirectional.

Seven into one

Palestinian embroidery designs are built up from a large collection of mainly geometrical border patterns, and the various combinations that can be used give them their distinctive appearance and never-ending interest. For this bag, seven patterns have been put together in the style of a Ramallah dress back panel. These patterns consist of three narrow framing borders (Figs 106a, b, c) while the remaining four are slightly wider (Figs 106d, e, f, g). Fig 106d is known as a half-opened bud pattern; Fig 106e is a stylised flower border; Fig 106f is a palm leaf or date palms. The back panel of a Ramallah dress usually consists of the date palm motif, joined together and worked to form a solid panel of embroidery with other borders framing it top and bottom, along the sides and continuing well above the main panel. Although black and dark blue are the colours most commonly used for clothing in the rest of the country, unbleached cottons and linens are favoured in Ramallah, and while red embroidery dominates on black and dark blue cloth, rust-red embroidery with a little black and green are the colours most used on calicos and linens. In keeping with this tradition, the bag is made from heavy calico and duck; the patterns stitched in terracotta, rust and black over a 6 threads/cm (15 threads/in) double-thread canvas which was later withdrawn.

130

FIG 106 Seven borders in bag
pattern
a, b, c framing borders
d, e, f, g slightly wider
borders

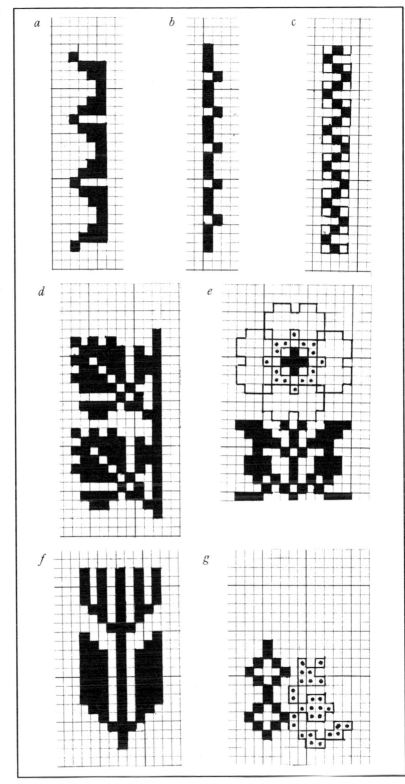

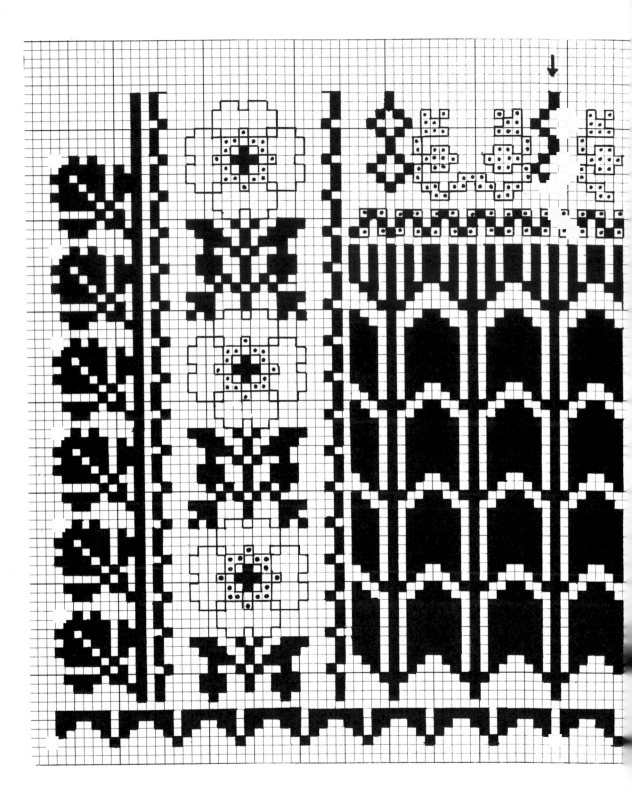

FIG 107 Bag pattern

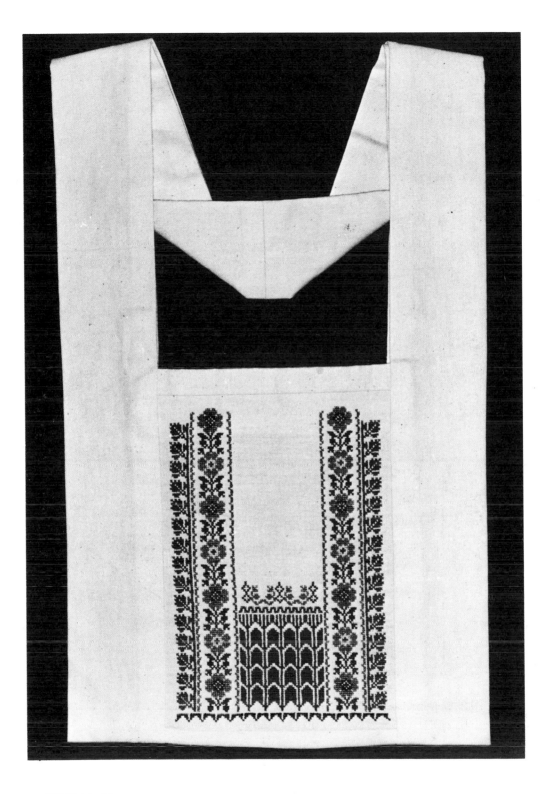

FIG 108 Finished bag

Spot motifs

Spot motifs can range from small geometrical patterns to much larger free embroidery forms. Sometimes the whole field is made up of one motif, or two motifs may alternate. Sometimes, if the motif is not symmetrical, it may face first to the left and then to the right. The collection of spot motifs from Yugoslavian headscarves (Fig 109) is

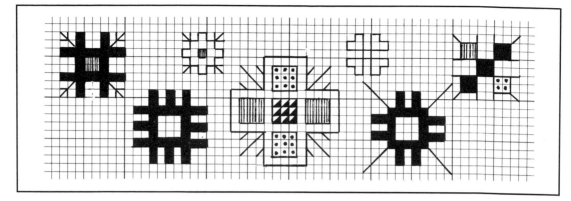

FIG 109 Spot motifs from Yugoslavian head scarves

FIG 110 Skull cap from North India, worked in fine crewel wool on cotton in chain stitch and rows of machine stitching

FIG 111 Diagram of cap

very simple, yet can be repeated and arranged to make attractive ground patterns. In colour photo 19 a spot motif of a carnation from Armenia has been used in this way. The interest lies in the colour variations, while in colour photo 20 spot motifs and borders have been combined to make a pattern. In both cases the motifs were stitched over canvas that was later removed.

Counted spot motifs stitched over canvas can be scattered over fine muslins and clothing materials just as easily as free work motifs. A very simple chain stitch motif surrounded by lines of stitching would be suitable for cushions, bags, pockets and yokes (Figs 110, 111).

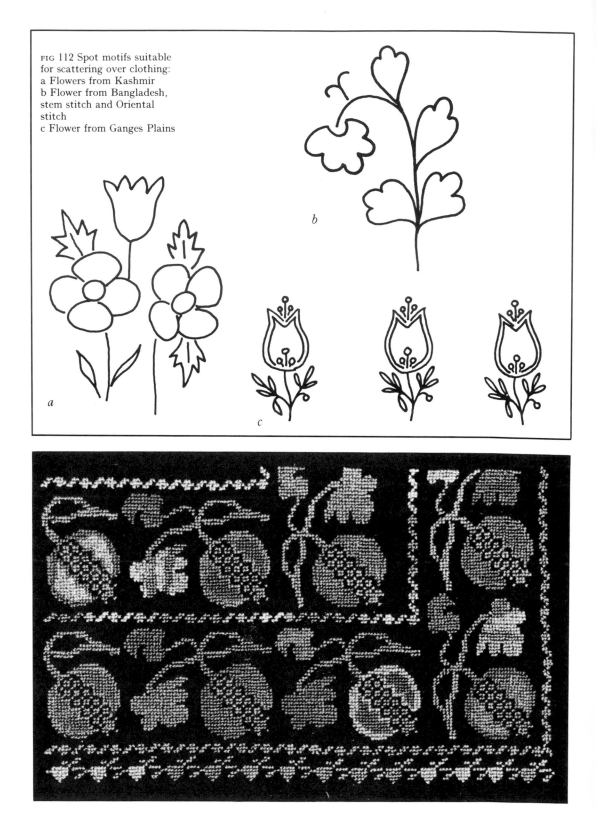

FIG 112 Spot motifs suitable for scattering over clothing:
a Flowers from Kashmir
b Flower from Bangladesh, stem stitch and Oriental stitch
c Flower from Ganges Plains

Bag of pomegranates

Sometimes you have a small practice piece of embroidery which is too good to discard, or you may have a fragment from an older embroidery that you treasure and would like to use. The little bag has been made up from half a Palestinian chest panel. The fragment measures 25cm × 15cm (10in × 6in) but the size is not important. It was worked over canvas on black cotton fabric in reds, orange, blues and dull yellow green. The pattern is made up of two narrow borders (Figs 88c, d) and a spot motif (Fig 114) used like a large border. The bag is finished with small beads and tassels.

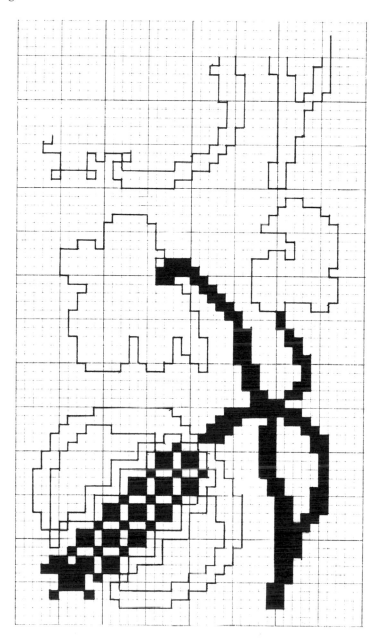

FIG 113 Copy of the original chest panel fragment

FIG 114 The pomegranate motif

Flower border bag

The edging of the ari shown in the colour photograph is made up of border upon border, and one of these has been used for this bag. The brown cotton used for the ari has itself been surrounded by a border of tan cotton. In keeping with this theme, two strips of cotton material, charcoal and dull khaki, have been sewn to the brown cotton of the bag. The pattern in chain stitch has been embroidered over these strips of material, using two strands of stranded cotton. The pattern given is the actual size and the finished bag measures 41cm × 30cm (16in × 12in) but again the size of the bag is not critical. By its very nature, a running border can run on for ever.

FIG 115 Bag embroidered
with border from Indian ari

FIG 116 Detail of embroidery

FIG 117 Diagram of border

138

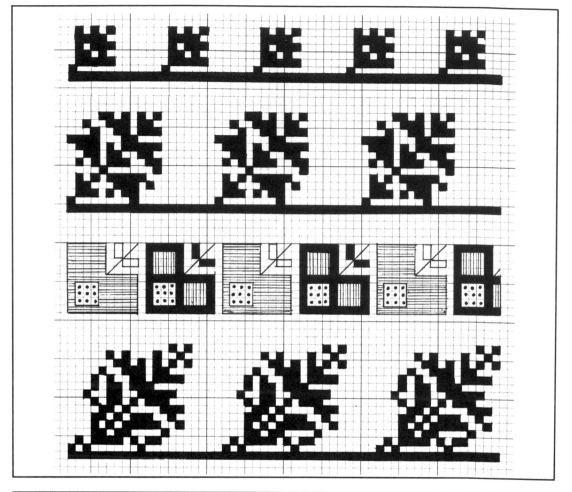

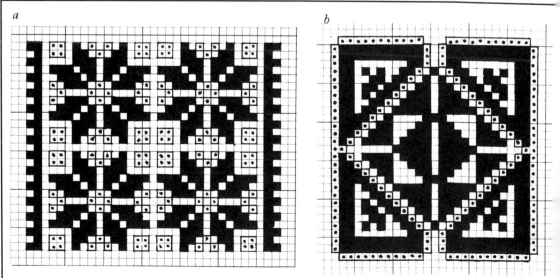

FIG 118 Running borders
and a border of spot motifs:
a Small running border from
Morocco
b Larger running border
from Morocco
c Spot motif from
Yugoslavia
d Large running border from
Morocco

FIG 119 Embroidered belt
from Palestine with all-over
pattern in cross stitch

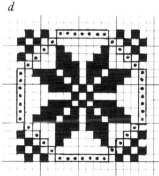

c

d

FIG 120 Non-directional
patterns:
a Belt pattern in red and
black cross stitch
b From cloth in red and
black cross stitch
c From cloth in red with
green or yellow in cross
stitch
d From cloth in red with
squares of green, purple,
yellow, blue

10 The stitches

Many of the stitches used in ethnic embroidery look familiar, although some of them may be worked in a slightly different way. A few, however, are almost unknown. Stitches must be pleasant and quick to work. When mastering a new stitch, use a heavy thread; some stitches are quite complex and this will help to show their construction more clearly. A different emphasis can be given to a stitch if the direction in which it is worked is suddenly changed. This happens frequently in cross stitch embroidery worked in one colour, where a change in direction of the slope of the stitch gives an illusion of a lighter or darker shade, depending on which way the light catches it. The direction in which the needle points also alters the construction of the stitch. While stitches are commonly worked with the needle pointing towards the worker, in some countries the needle is pointed away from the worker. Just as there are different stitches, there are often different ways of working the same stitch. The stitches illustrated are either relatively unknown or used in a different way.

Back stitch

A stitch commonly used in sewing, for outlines and quilting, but here used as a filling stitch. Back stitches should be small and regular.

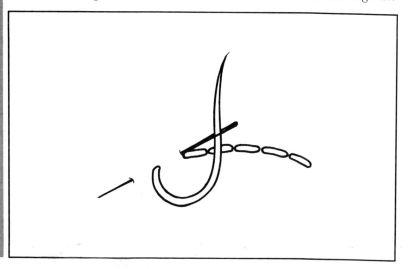

FIG 121 Back stitch

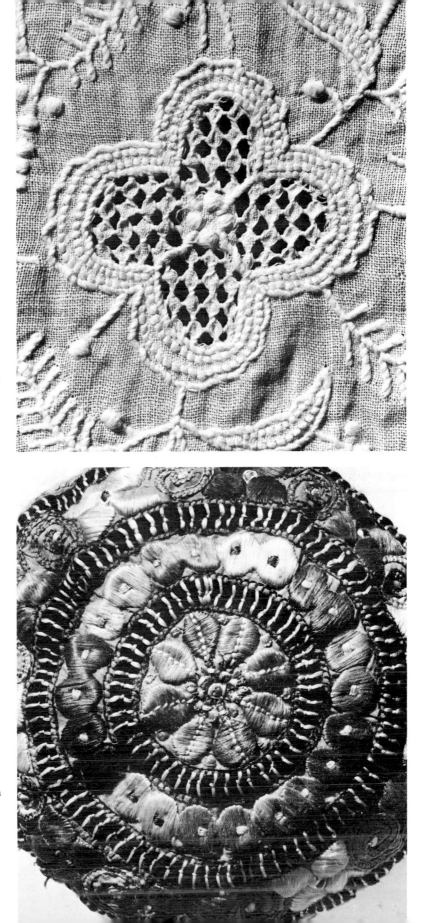

FIG 122 Enlarged detail of a piece of whitework thought to have been embroidered in Ireland but bearing a strong resemblance to *Chikankari*. Embroidered with white cotton thread on very fine muslin. Late nineteenth century

FIG 123 Crown of Pathan cap, north-west India, worked with silk floss on cotton. Back stitch is used to control the silk floss satin stitch while being decorative. Mid twentieth century

Chain stitch

This stitch can be used either as an outline or a filling stitch. As a filling it can be used to simply follow the basic outline or in such a way that it indicates contours.

FIG 124 Chain stitch

FIG 125 Detail of a trade fabric, worked with crewel wool on Dusatti, showing chain stitch used as a filling stitch, following the outline. Ari work

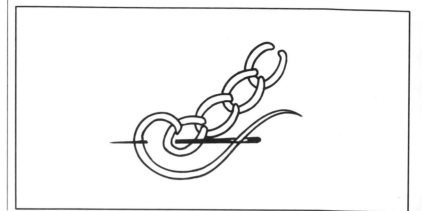

FIG 126 Detail from an
Egyptian embroidery, silk
on rough handwoven linen,
showing the stitch worked in
such a way that body
contours are indicated.
Early twentieth century

FIG 127 Enlarged detail from
a Persian embroidery, fine
silk thread on corded silk,
showing motif outlined in
chain stitch but the chain
stitch filling independent of
the outline. Early twentieth
century

a

b

c

FIG 128 Chikan stem stitch

Chikan stem stitch

When Chikan work is described, the stems and outlines are invariably given as worked in stem stitch. Stem stitch would be almost impossible to work satisfactorily given the weight of thread used and the fineness of the muslin. Actually, the stems and outlines are worked like a single row of laid Oriental stitch. When the stitch is completed, the small slanting stitches are indistinguishable from the laid thread in slope and size. (In this stitch, the needle will be pointing towards the worker either when the thread is laid down or on the return journey. Find the way which is the most comfortable to work at speed.) Make a stitch (in Chikan work this should be no longer than 1cm) by bringing the thread to the surface and about 2.5cm (1in) above this point make a small stitch with the needle pointing towards you and the thread on the left(a). Pull the laid stitch flat (b) and working from right to left, couch down the laid thread (c). If the needle is placed under the laid thread almost straight, and not on a slant as you would normally do for couching, the completed stitch will look like a row of stem stitch. To make a longer stem, make a succession of small stitches the required length of the stem, then couch the whole line at once.

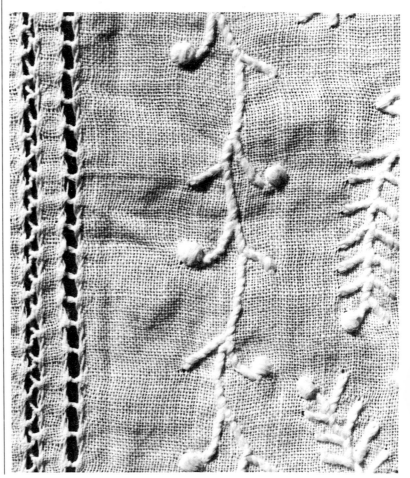

FIG 129 Enlarged detail from piece of white work, white cotton on fine white muslin. Late nineteenth century

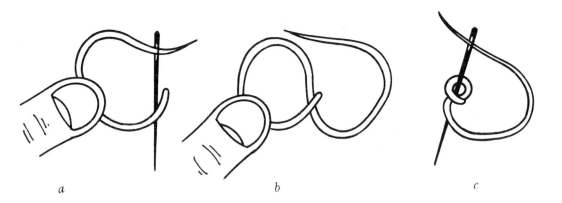

a   b   c

FIG 130 Chinese knot

FIG 131 Enlarged detail of a tree peony worked in silk floss and outlined with a couched gold thread. Late nineteenth century

Chinese knot

This stitch is used extensively in Chinese embroidery both as a knot and as a filling stitch. When it is used as a filling stitch, it is worked in rows from right to left following the outline of the motif. Before the needle is pulled through the material (c), the knot is tightened on the needle. This makes a very regular and much neater knot than a French knot.

10. End of a bolster worked
in silk floss on calico in cross
stitch and plait stitch. It is
made up of a tree of life
border, two geometrical
borders and a running
border. Morocco, late
nineteenth century

11. Small bag made from
half a chest panel of two
small borders and a
pomegranate motif. For
hundreds of years the
pomegranate motif has been
stitched on to household
linens both in cross stitch
and free work. Middle East,
mid twentieth century

Long-tailed Chinese knot

This is a variation of the Chinese knot and much less common. The knot is worked in the same way but the stitch under the fabric to make the next stitch is longer and slopes to the right, just under the previous knot.

FIG 132 Detail from an embroidery of long-tailed Chinese knot worked in silk floss and outlined with couched gold. Late nineteenth century

150

Couching

Couching is a method of tying down one or more threads with another, usually thinner, thread, in either the same or a contrasting colour. It can be used for outlines or as a filling. It is useful for attaching heavy and metallic threads and also for tying down floating silk floss threads in the simplest forms of laid work. Usually the couching thread is placed at right angles to the laid thread, but with the heavy corded thread used in Bethlehem embroidery the couching lies with the twist of the cord and so is inconspicuous. (a) couching with Oriental stitch, (b) Bethlehem couching with the twist of the thread, (c) another type of couching on the Bethlehem dress in the style of Turkish Kordon stitch.

FIG 133a Couching with Oriental stitch
b Bethlehem couching
c Turkish-type couching

FIG 134 Detail from an appliquéd Indian wall-hanging of a horse and rider. The outline has been edged with a couched thread and emphasis has been given to part of the motif by a thread couched on top of the appliquéd piece. Mid twentieth century

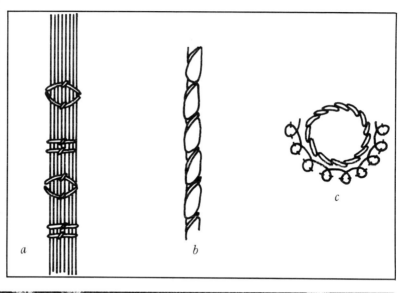

12. End of sleeve, Bethlehem Wedding dress. The sleeve, like the dress is made from strips of red and tan silk. The joins are covered with silk floss stitches. The embroidery is in couched gilt and silk cords and is surmounted by a strange bird, suggesting that it is perhaps yet another form of the tree of life motif. Bethlehem, 1910

13. Detail from a cloth. Raw silk embroidered in silk floss in stem stitch and Oriental stitch. Pattern flowing along an undulating line and turning back to fill the empty space. Kashmir, mid twentieth century

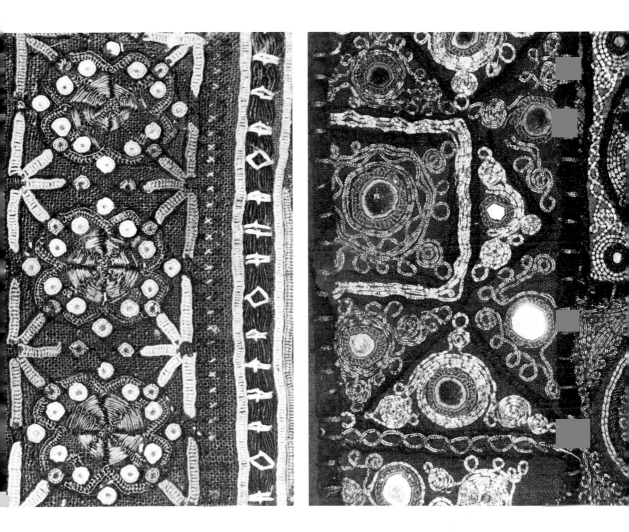

FIG 135 Detail from the back panel of a Bethlehem wedding dress. The motif is made up of straight and looped cords in metallic threads, yellow green, mauve, with small amounts of satin stitch filling in cyclamen and grey green. 1910

FIG 136 Detail from a fragment of chest panel of groups of threads couched with Oriental stitch. India, mid twentieth century

FIG 137 Detail from a *chakla* made from recycled clothing of *shisha* glass and couched metallic threads. The joins are covered by a heavy couching thread typical of Kutch work. Mid twentieth century

14. Detail from sleeve band, polycoloured floss silk on dark orange damask weave silk. The embroidery is unfinished and shows the traced outlines of the design. It is often difficult to distinguish between magnolia, lotus and tree peony flowers. This particular flower has the pointed petals of the lotus, but the leaves are unquestionably magnolia. Late nineteenth century

15. Detail from a sleeve band embroidered with both silk floss and twisted silk thread. Facial details have been stitched over the floss using a finer thread to give some modelling. The laid silk floss in the skirt has been couched in the hemp leaves pattern. The sleeve bands varied in width from 7 to 13cm (3 to 5 inches). The length was approximately 112cm (44 inches), of which half was embroidered. This was the part that was seen when the arms were folded in front of the body. China, late nineteenth century

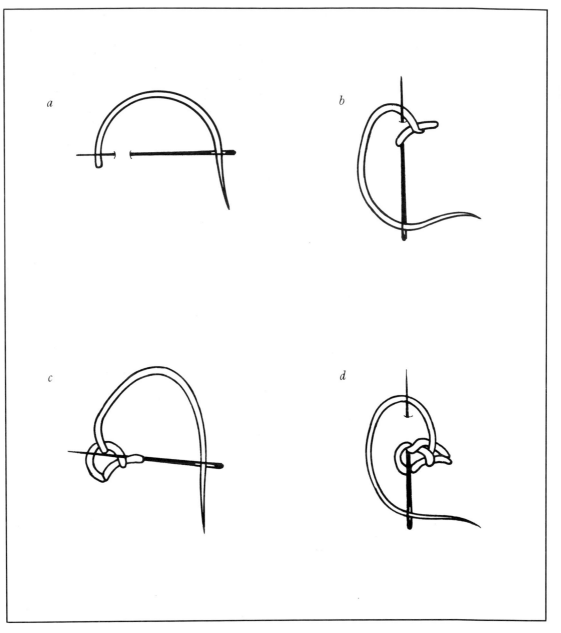

FIG 138 Indian edging

Indian edging stitch

This edging is closely related to *shisha* stitch. Work this stitch away from you. Bring the thread to the surface and slightly above and to the right make a small stitch with the thread under the needle (a). With the thread under the needle make a stitch with the needle pointing away from you (b). Beside stitch (a) make another stitch (c). With the thread under the needle make a stitch similar to (b). Continue from (a). The detached chain stitches are put in on a second working. The other variations has two rows of small beads instead of the detached chain and an extra row of chain stitch.

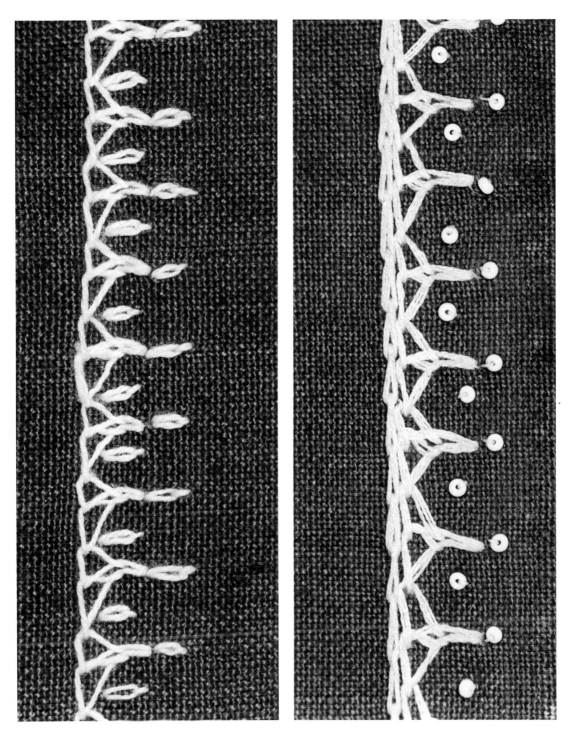

FIG 139 Enlarged detail of
edging with detached chain
stitch

FIG 140 Enlarged detail of
another version of Indian
edging with row of white
beads. India, mid twentieth
century

16. Sleeve band of flowers including magnolia in encroaching satin stitch with voiding between the petals and tree peony in Chinese knots. Also on the band are the endless knot, one of the Eight Buddhist Emblems of Happy Augury and the coins, one of the Eight Precious Things. China, late nineteenth century

17. Blouse

Murri stitch

Murri is the name for the grains of rice in Chikan embroidery. With the needle pointing towards you, make an unequal-sided chain stitch (a). Take the needle down through the material a short distance below the chain stitch (b). Bring the needle to the surface in the middle of this stitch with the thread on the right, and slip the needle under the small stitch at the base of the chain from right to left (c). Work straight satin stitches over this padding along the length of the grain, beginning at the widest part of the padding.

FIG 141 Murri stitch

FIG 142 Detail from a piece of *Chikankari* worked in white cotton on fine white muslin. Ganges Plains, mid twentieth century

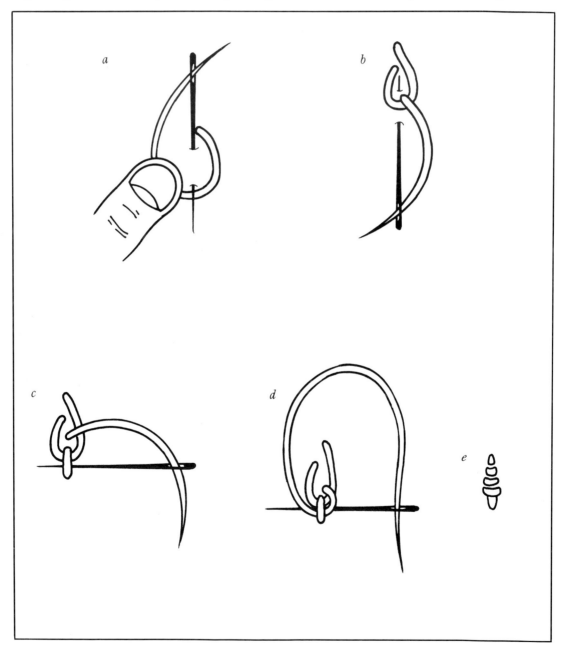

18. Detail of satin stitch
embroidery in silk floss on
handwoven linen over a unit
of four threads. The pattern
is made up of one motif
repeated in such a way as to
suggest weaving. Zagreb,
Yugoslavia, late nineteenth
century

19. Spot motif bag,
Carnations in a Field,
25cm × 28cm (10 × 11 inches)
Armenian motif

Oriental stitch

This stitch is also known as Romanian stitch and Indian filling stitch. It is used extensively, as it covers the ground quickly with little wasted thread on the back. While this stitch is usually worked as a filling stitch, it may also be worked singly to tie down a couched thread.

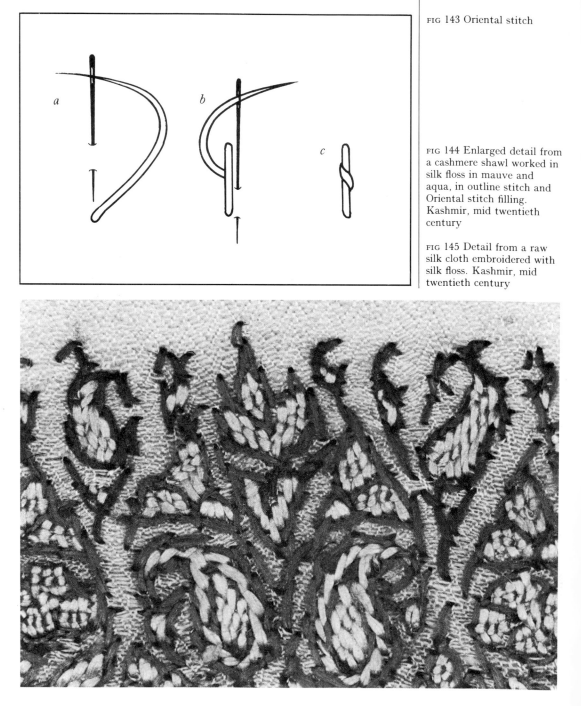

FIG 143 Oriental stitch

FIG 144 Enlarged detail from a cashmere shawl worked in silk floss in mauve and aqua, in outline stitch and Oriental stitch filling. Kashmir, mid twentieth century

FIG 145 Detail from a raw silk cloth embroidered with silk floss. Kashmir, mid twentieth century

20. Bag of spot motifs and
borders. Armenian motif

FIG 146 Detail from a chest
panel worked on black
taffeta. The entire panel is
covered in stitching, mostly
shisha stitch and Oriental
stitch worked in blocks of
artificial silk floss, fine purl
silk, cotton and waving
threads in a riot of colour;
white, Turkey red, orange,
rust, dark blue, yellow, and
yellow green. India

Outline stitch

This is a form of stem stitch used in Kashmiri embroidery, often in conjunction with Oriental stitch. It is worked like a long stem stitch, but with the thread on the left of the needle. With stem stitch, the size of the stitch is reduced at a sharp point, here it is exaggerated and tied down by the following stitch (c).

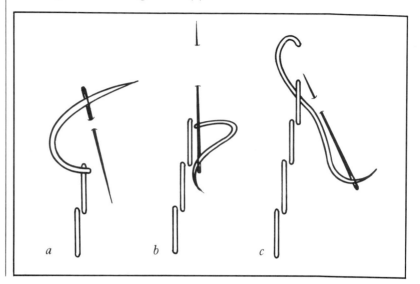

FIG 147 Outline stitch

FIG 148 Enlarged detail from a cashmere shawl embroidered in mauve and aqua silk floss in outline stitch and Oriental stitch, and showing the distinctive tips on the leaf motif. Kashmir, mid twentieth century

Pekinese stitch

This is used as a filling stitch in Chinese embroidery. Always work from the outline of the design towards the centre of the shape to be covered. Make a foundation row of back stitches. Into these back stitches lace a second thread. Since the interlaced thread does not enter the background material, it is a very suitable stitch for gold, silver and heavy threads. Recent research from China suggests that this stitch is 'couched' rather than 'laced'.

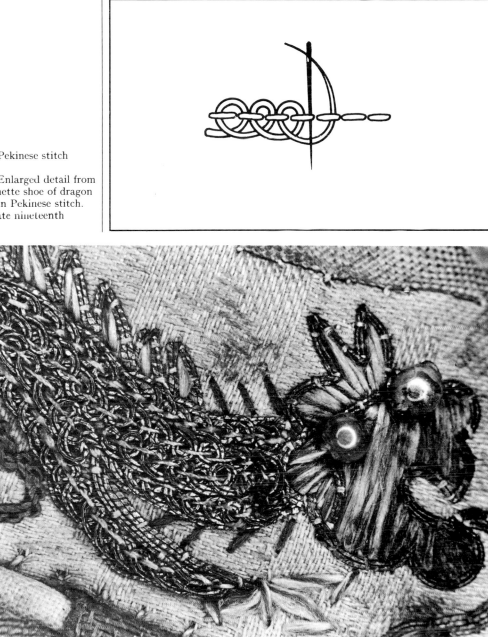

FIG 149 Pekinese stitch

FIG 150 Enlarged detail from a marionette shoe of dragon worked in Pekinese stitch. China, late nineteenth century

Phanda knot

Special stitches named after seed grains are a feature of Chikan embroidery. They are all built up over a chain or buttonhole stitch, Murri is the name of the grain of rice stitch, while the millet grain stitch is called Phanda knot. There is also another stitch made of small satin stitches over a tiny chain stitch which is often confused with Phanda knot and for want of a name has been called Grain stitch. To make Phanda knot, take a small slanting stitch towards the right and bring the needle out directly above it. Bring the needle down under the small slanting stitch (a). With the needle pointing away from you, make a buttonhole stitch on the slanting stitch (b) and slip this stitch to the top of the slanting stitch. Make a second buttonhole stitch (c). Put the needle into the fabric under the buttonhole stitch and out at the base of the knot (d). Anchor the stitch by slipping the needle under the small slanting stitch from left to right. Phanda knot is a tiny round stitch. If it is oval rather than round, check that you are tightening the buttonhole stitches sufficiently.

FIG 151 Phanda knot

FIG 152 Enlarged detail from a piece of Chikan work, white on white, of Chikan stem stitch, back stitch, Murri stitch and Phanda knot. Ganges Plains, mid twentieth century

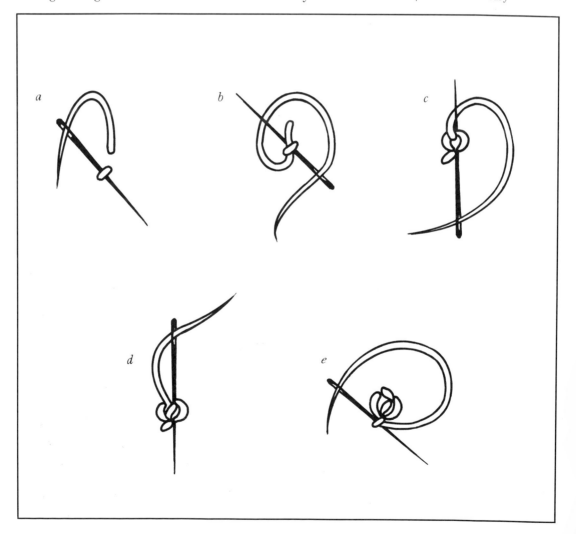

a

b

c

d

e

Grain stitch

Make a tiny chain stitch (a). Over this at right angles make three or four tiny satin stitches.

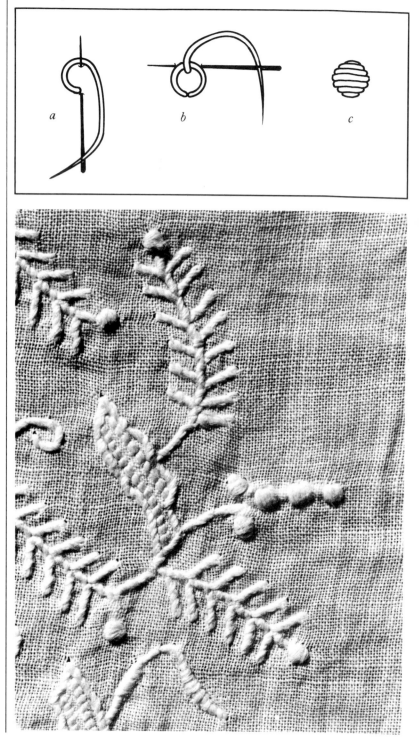

Plait stitch

Work from left to right. This stitch is easier to work if it is begun with an ordinary cross stitch (a). Bring the needle out at lower left corner and with the needle pointing towards you make a stitch (b), and complete the cross (c). This makes a more substantial stitch than cross stitch, and when a heavy thread is used the finished stitch looks like a plait. The back should show a row of upright parallel stitches.

FIG 155 Plait stitch

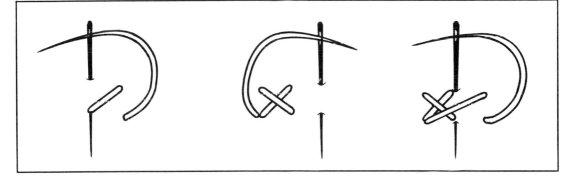

FIG 156 Enlarged detail of a tree of life motif showing cross stitch and plait stitch. The direction of the stitch in the centre of the tree has been deliberately changed for added emphasis. Morocco, late nineteenth century

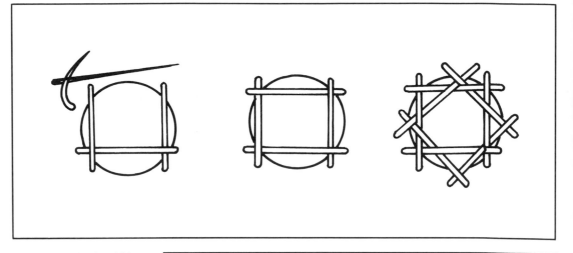

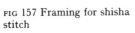

FIG 157 Framing for shisha
stitch

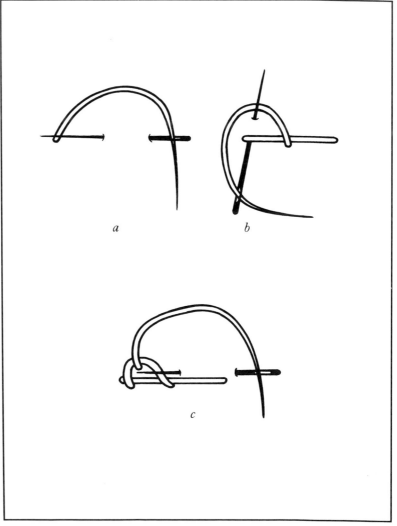

a   *b*

c

FIG 158 Shisha stitch

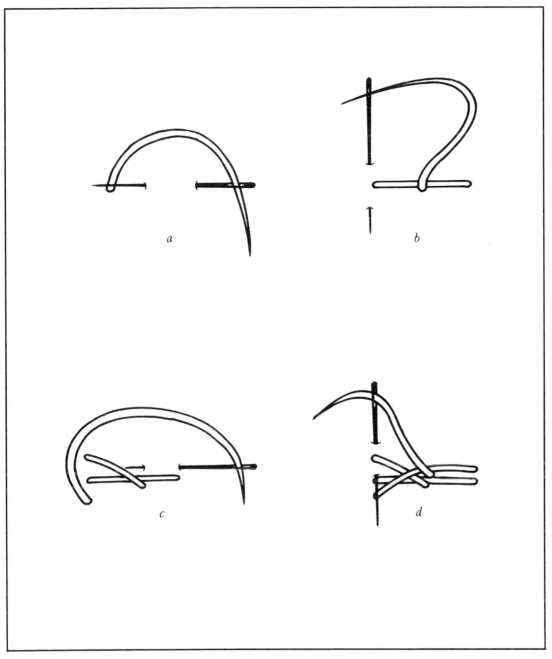

a

b

c

d

Shisha stitch

It is important that the shisha mirrors which are made of rough-edged glass are firmly attached to the background material. In this method the first four threads are locked into position by the second group of four threads. The stitches used to cover this framework vary but they are all based on a type of Cretan feather stitch. To get the slope of the stitch correct it needs to be worked away from you. The stitch is given in Fig 158, while Fig 159 shows a herringbone variation.

FIG 159 Herringbone variations of shisha stitch

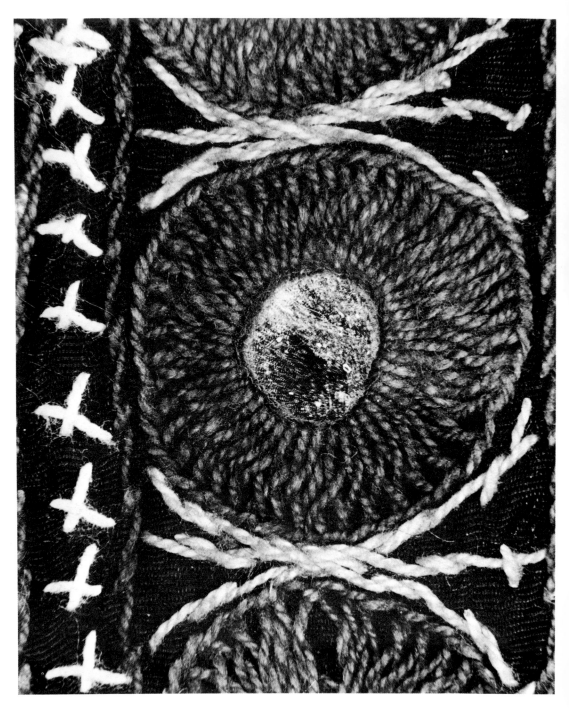

FIG 160 Enlarged detail of
shisha stitch from chest
panel. The stitch on its own
looks heavy and it is usually
softened with buttonhole
stitch, fly stitch or long
couched threads. India

FIG 161 Enlarged detail of
shisha stitch, softened with
long-tailed Chinese knots,
rows of fly stitch

FIG 162 Enlarged detail of
herringbone variation of
shisha stitch from an export
trade skirt. India, modern

Stroke stitch

This is a variation of double running stitch which runs in a zig-zag line.

FIG 163 Stroke stitch

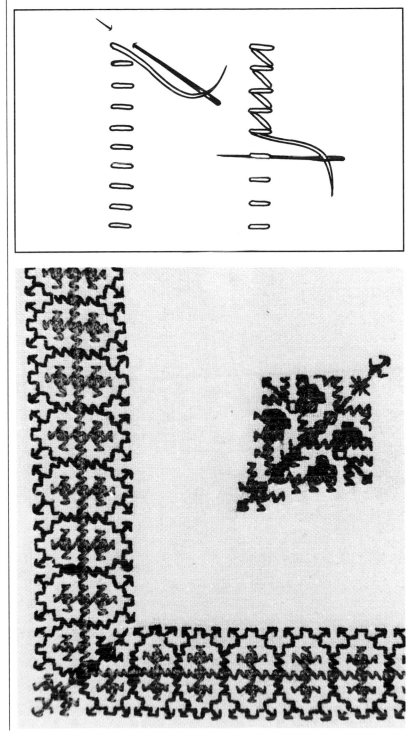

FIG 164 Detail from cloth of stroke stitch. Morocco, mid twentieth century

FIG 165 Enlarged detail from
cloth in stroke stitch

Turkmen stitch

This stitch resembles a closed feather stitch and is used as a quick,
economical filling. The stitch forms a characteristic ridge on either
side of the crossed filling. It is worked in Iran, by the semi-nomadic
Turkmen, in India and Pakistan. Bring the thread to the surface and
to the left, and below this point make a stitch with the thread under
the needle (a). Cross to the right and make a small stitch again with
the thread under the needle (b). Cross to the left, place the needle
between the crossed threads and make another small stitch (c).
Continue working from right to left.

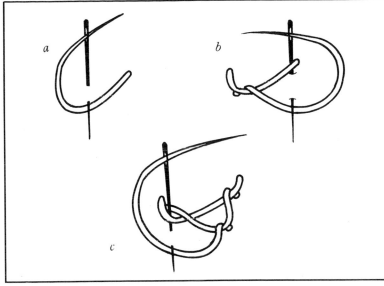

FIG 166 Turkmen stitch

FIG 167 Enlarged detail of Pathan cap worked in silk floss on yellow cotton, in chain stitch, Oriental stitch couching Yemeni knots and Turkmen stitch. North-west India, mid twentieth century

Yemeni knot

This knot stitch appears on both the Yemeni braces and the Pathan cap. It is made up of two or three buttonhole stitches. With the needle pointing towards you make a small buttonhole stitch (a). In the same hole at the top of the stitch and a fraction to the right at the bottom of the stitch, make another buttonhole stitch (b). Slip the needle into the fabric under the second stitch and away from you.

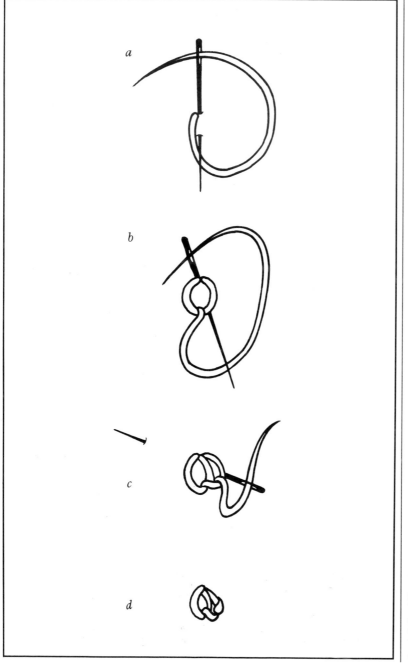

a

b

c

d

FIG 168 Yemeni knot

FIG 169 Enlarged detail of braces, worked in chain stitch, couched metallic thread and Yemeni knots. Yemen, mid twentieth century

Suppliers

Names of specific retail shops can be found in *Embroidery*, the magazine published quarterly by The Embroiderers' Guild, Apartment 41, Hampton Court Palace, East Molesey, Surrey KT8 9AU. This magazine also covers a wide range of embroidery topics and news. The Royal School of Needlework, 5 King Street, London WC2 8HN can supply a wide range of books, fabrics and threads.

The following firms will give lists of local stockists on request.

Appleton Bros Ltd
Church Street
Chiswick, London W4

Coats Domestic Marketing Division
39 Durham Street
Glasgow G41 1BS

DMC UK Distributors
Dunlicraft Ltd
Pullman Road
Wigston
Leicester LE8 2DY

Gütermann-Perivale
Wadsworth Road
Greenford
Middlesex UB6 7JS

Madeira Threads (UK) Ltd
Ryder House
Back Lane
Boroughbridge
North Yorkshire

C.M. Offray and Son Ltd (Ribbons)
Fir Tree Place
Church Road
Ashford
Middlesex TW15 2PH

Paterna Persian Yarn
NeedleArt House
P.O. Box 13
Albion Mills
Wakefield WF2 9SG

Index